DANIEL GEFEN

#1 International Best-Seller

THE SELF HELP ADDICT

TURN AN
OVERDOSE OF
INFORMATION
INTO A LIFE OF
TRANSFORMATION

DANIEL GEFEN

By (c) Copyright
All rights reserved.
Book Layout ©2018
www.EvolveGlobalPublishing.com

No part of this book may be reproduced or transmitted in any form or by any means, electronic or mechanical, including photocopying, recording or by any information storage and retrieval system, without written permission from the authors, except for the inclusion of brief quotations in a review.

Limit of Liability Disclaimer: The information contained in this book is for information purposes only, and may not apply to your situation. The author, publisher, distributor and provider provide no warranty about the content or accuracy of content enclosed. Information provided is subjective. Keep this in mind when reviewing this guide. Neither the Publisher nor Authors shall be liable for any loss of profit or any other commercial damages resulting from the use of this guide. All links are for information purposes only and are not warranted for content, accuracy, or any other implied or explicit purpose.

Earnings Disclaimer: All income examples in this book are just that – examples. They are not intended to represent or guarantee that everyone will achieve the same results. You understand that each individual's success will be determined by his or her desire, dedication, background, effort and motivation to work. There is no guarantee you will duplicate any of the results stated here. You recognize any business endeavours has inherent risk or loss of capital.

The Self Help Addict

1st Edition. 2018
ASIN: B078KKLJ8C (Amazon Kindle)
ISBN-10: 1981930450 (Amazon Print)
ISBN-13: 978-1981930456 (Amazon Print)
ISBN: 978-1-64204-571-0 (Ingram Spark) PAPERBACK
ISBN: 978-1-64204-572-7 (Ingram Spark) HARDCOVER
ISBN-13: 978-1981930456 (CreateSpace)
ISBN-10: 1981930450 (CreateSpace)
ISBN: 9781370857371 (Smashwords)

CONTACT THE AUTHOR:
Business Name: Gefen Media Group
Author Website: www.DanielGefen.com
Main Website: www.TheSelfHelpAddict.com
LinkedIn: https://www.linkedin.com/in/gefenmedia
Email: Daniel@TheSelfHelpAddict.com

TRADEMARKS

All product names, logos, and brands are the property of their respective owners. All company, product and service names used in this book are for identification purposes only. Use of these names, logos, and brands does not imply endorsement. All other trademarks cited herein are the property of their respective owners.

Fonts we used in the layout: Univers Roman
Book Size: 6x9

Acknowledgements

If I try to thank everyone I will need the length of this book.

I try to consider everyone I meet to be a friend and I consider my friends as part of my extended family.

So to all my extended family, thank you.

Thank you to David Greenfield for the editing of this book, John North for publishing, Jacob Schwartz for the cover design, Brian Spector for the photoshoot and everyone involved in helping me make this book happen.

Thank you to Rabbi Gerzi for being my spiritual guide and teaching me how to be a humble servant and that it's better to be happy than right.

To my siblings: Yoel, Bracha, and Benjy. I love each of you more than I may have the courage to express.

To my parents: Thank you for being proud. It's worth more to me than all the awards in the world.

To my dear children: Elisha, Gabriel, Freida and Ori. Each of you bring a whole world of joy to my life. There is nothing you can do to diminish the amount of love I have for you.

To my precious queen: The most important person in my life.

My beautiful wife, words can't describe what I want to express. I am nothing without you and everything with you. I didn't write this book. WE did.

Thank you to my Creator. May this book bring more light to your children.

Table of Contents

Introduction 1
What is a self help addict? 7
My Story 13
Less Information
    What Do You REALLY Want? 37
    Play The Long Game 41
    Take Full Control 45
    Go From Consumer To Creator 49
    Think Less, Do More 57
    Be Persistent 65
    Make Fear Your Friend 73
    The Paradox Of Choice 77
    Commit Distraction Suicide 83
    Man/Woman The Heck Up 91
    Pain Is Your Friend 95
    Get Comfortable With Being Uncomfortable 101
    Abundance VS Scarcity Mindset 107
    Rewrite Your Script 113
    Ups And Downs 119
    Keeping Things In Perspective 129

Becoming a Superhero 137

Be Memorable 141

Be Yourself (everyone else is already taken) 149

Create a Nation

Find Your 1000 True Fans 157

Become a Super Connector 163

Successful Creators 169

Write Your Own Book 175

Launch Your Own Podcast 185

Transformation

Being and Becoming 195

The Power Of Silence 205

Lefkowitz and Feldman 209

Your Roots Are Your Foundation 215

Final Thoughts 219

About The Author 221

Introduction

"Checkmate, dad."

With a twinkle in his eye and a smile from ear to ear my eight-year-old son, Elisha declared that he had finally beaten me in chess. This was one of those proud moments a father feels when his son has outdone him.

As a little boy, all I wanted was to make my father proud. That little boy seems to have been residing within me all these years and deep down inside his desire to 'prove himself' has driven me all my life.

At the age of 33, I feel as if the desire to make my son proud is of equal importance if not greater.

Today I told my first born son that for his tenth birthday, his daddy is going to publish a book.

"What kind of book?" He asked excitedly. "Will there be dragons in it?"

I chuckled because, in a way, there are dragons in this book. These dragons are the fiery obstacles known as *fear*, and its accomplices *doubt* and *indecision* that keep us from becoming the best we can be.

"No, it isn't a storybook. It's a book that will hopefully help many people get out of their own way and accomplish more."

I can see my son's eyes squint and the light wrinkles on his forehead with a little confusion.

"You will understand what the book is about one day." I assured him. "I just want to let you know that the first copy I print will be for you on your tenth birthday."

He smiled and his face returned to its glowing innocence and he kissed me goodnight.

Elisha, this book is written for you. It's a gift that I wish someone gave me when I was a young boy.

It's a book about how **self doubt**, **procrastination**, and **indecision** create a cycle what many people in this world are trapped in.

It's a book about how people search long and hard for **a secret key that doesn't exist**.

It's a book about how people often invest their time, energy and money in self-help books, courses, events and come out the other end still feeling **unaccomplished**.

It's a book about how you can **make your fears your friend** and achieve anything your heart desires.

It's a book about the importance of always **taking responsibility** for what happens in your life and **taking control** of your outcomes.

It's a book about how much **abundance** there is in this world and that there is enough money, love and happiness for everyone to have a lifetime supply.

It's a book about **going from a consumer to a creator**.

It's a book about **taking action**, because without action, nothing gets done.

It's a book about setting deadlines and **becoming accountable** so you avoid putting things off.

It's a book about **choosing your friends wisely** because you become the average of the people you surround yourself with.

Introduction

It's a book about the power of **decisiveness** and how to avoid feeling overwhelmed.

It's a book about how **you already have everything you need**.

It's a book about the importance of having an **attitude of gratitude**.

It's a book about the importance of **living in the moment for the moment**.

It's a book about **getting high and staying high** (without drugs).

It's a book about the importance of **having structure in your life**.

It's a book about **being and becoming**.

It's a book about why **you have already won**.

It's a book about how the real hero, that you have searched so long and hard for, is **you**.

Okay, so here goes.

Believe it or not, it has taken me over 10 years to start writing this book (how ironic). I have thought about writing this book constantly, but every time I sat down to type, I just made so many excuses why I couldn't.

I was overthinking.

All the things that could go wrong.

It needs to be perfect.

What should I write first?

Then one day I finally sat down and just started typing. I decided that the war in my head was going to stop. I was going to write this book and nothing in my head was going to talk me out of it.

In fact, the very reason I decided to write this book is because of the countless times I have held myself back over the last 10 years. Nothing kills procrastination as much as taking major action. This book you are holding in your hands is a living testament that I live by the advice I give in this book (well, I try my best to, anyway :)).

My obsession with bookstores (before the days of Amazon)

Growing up, I was addicted to self-help.

I would go into Barnes & Noble and get lost in the self-help aisle trying to find 'the right book'. You know what I mean when I say 'the right book' - it has to jump out at you.

I would end up with a stack of about 10 and then start flicking through.

First I would look at the front cover then move to the back cover and then the testimonials and then at the contents section.

Ooh, that looks good. I'll read one chapter.

I lost track of time and space. Completely forgetting where I was and the fact that my wife and kids were waiting outside. Until finally, I would find 'the right book' "Yeah, this is it. This is the one." As I would go to pay for it there would be this little voice inside saying, "I have a feeling that this is the book that's going to change my life. This is the one. I'm going to read this book and that's it. It's all going to be good now."

I would read the book with my yellow highlighter in hand highlighting away every line that leapt out at me. Wow. That's so amazing. That's Life Changing. Wow that's going to change my life.

Introduction

And then I would get to the end of the book, and there would be this sense of fear.

What now?

I've read the whole book. Now what do I do?

While I'm reading the book, I have an excuse not to do anything because I'm reading the book. I'm in training. I'm gathering information. I'm in learning mode. So nobody can expect me to do anything. I'm still gaining the knowledge.

But, then when you get to the end of the book, you've got no more excuses. You've ran out of rope. Now, you're like, "Uh oh. I've got to take action. Crap. I'm scared."

"Oh, no. I can't do this."

What do you do? A self-help addict will do this.

Go to the author's website.

Oh, look at all this information. I need this information.

Oh, look. They've got a webinar coming out. I've got to go to this webinar. If I go to the webinar, then they're going to tell me and explain to me exactly what I need to do and you go to the webinar.

They tell you at the end of the webinar that they've got this big event in Vegas. And, if you come to the event, then your life will change. Then you're like, "Oh my god. That's exactly what I need." But you don't have the money. I'll borrow the money. I'll steal the money. I'll find it because if I go to this event, then I'm going to change.

To cut a long story short, it's a never-ending cycle - you end up with another book and you end up following another author. It's the same thing with diets, and it's the same thing with business ideas, and it's the same thing with everything else you do.

I wrote this book to show you how to break the cycle.

What is a Self-help Addict?

Like so many others, I have read tons of self-help books, listened to hours and hours of audio-books and attended countless seminars. Ultimately, however, I was just reading one book after the other without making any significant changes in my life.

I see this pattern happening to so many others. I believe there is a new-age addiction. Many people suffer from this addiction without even realizing they are addicted.

This addiction is so powerful that you persuade yourself that it is good for you. Each and every self-help book is going to "change your life." Every diet program is going to be the last one. The one that you will stick to and finally get you to your goal weight.

"This business seminar is worth every penny because I am going to learn how to become rich from it."

This addiction plagues our generation because we live in a world where things have become so easy. We don't need to work to build a fire for warmth or light.

We can have things at the touch of a button. This has created a quick-fix mentality whereby we think that someone is going to tell us how to lose weight or make millions in weeks — and we believe them. Then when it doesn't happen, we tell ourselves that we just need to read another book, listen to another audio, or go to another exciting seminar.

We are fooling ourselves.

We have become Self-help Addicts.

Self-help addiction is a never-ending cycle of highs and lows created by hype, hope, and laziness.

We have been sold and then sold again and we will continue to be sold as long as we buy into it. We will keep opening our wallets and wasting time listening to recycled and repackaged information until we stop and realize what is happening.

We have become escape artists. Lost in social media messages. Lost in Youtube videos. Lost in reality TV shows. Lost in bits of data. We have plugged ourselves into the matrix and simultaneously unplugged ourselves from reality. We have become machines. Responding to pings and tweets obsessively and compulsively. We have become reactive to hundreds or thousands of daily interruptions. We have given away our attention to "others" to the detriment of our most loved ones. We have been robbed of our most precious asset.

Time.

This book was written to help you break out of the cycle and achieve things you didn't believe possible.

My goal is to help you go from an overdose of information to a life of transformation.

This book is for those of you who really want to change.

If you really want to make more money, become healthier, improve your relationships and go from consumer to creator then this will be the last self-help book you ever need to read. (unless, of course, I decide to write another book :))

Let's Bake A Cake!

Like anything in life, the difference between two things is what they are made up of.

What is a self help addict?

If I bake two cakes with the same ingredients using the same measurements and at the same temperature for the same time in the same oven, I will have identical cakes. But if I change the ingredients any one of those factors — the ingredients, measurements, temperature, or time then I will end up with different cakes.

Self-help Addicts consist (for the most part) of similar ingredients. To become a Successful Leader we first need to look at what ingredients they share.

After picking the brains of over 100 super achievers on my podcast show, I have come to discover the reason for their incredible accomplishments.

They are not trapped in the self-help addiction cycle. I have included some of them in this book as examples of what it could be like once you escape the self-made prison of self-help addiction.

These guests include the smartest man in the world, the leading hostage negotiator for the FBI, business tycoons, celebrity influencers, and thought leaders.

Some of the common ingredients Self-help Addicts suffer from:

Indecisive, Overwhelmed, Self Doubt, Paralyzed by Fear, Low Self Esteem, Procrastination, Impatience, Perfectionism, Self Inflicted Mental/ Emotional Abuse, Information Over Consumption, Follow the Leader Mentality, Idolize the Hero Syndrome, Overcomplicating and Overanalyzing things, Highly Risk Averse, Inconsistency, Scarcity Mindset, Stuck in the Details, Spends Time with other Self-help Addicts, Blames Others, Lacks Accountability, Unstructured, Neglects their Health, Relies on Substances to Get 'High'.

Some of the common ingredients of Successful Leaders:

Decisive, Focused, Self Confidence, Courageous, High Self Worth, Seizes the Moment, Patience, Gets Things Done, Has a 'Good is Good Enough' Attitude, Self Accepting, Efficient Time Management, LEads Others, Plays to Their Strengths and Delegates Their Weaknesses, Gets Inspiration from other Super Achievers, Keeps Things Simple, Takes Calculated Risks, Maintains Consistency, Abundance Mindset, Sees the Big Picture while Living in the Moment, Spends Time with other Super Achievers , Takes 100% Responsibility, Hold Themselves Accountable to others, Has Structure, Maintains Good Balanced Health, Gets Natural Highs.

In this book, I will lay out these ingredients and if you bake the right cake you should be able to go from Self-help Addict to Successful Leader.

DISCLAIMER:

I am *not* saying that the consumption of self-help material is bad. I have gained tremendously from the self-help industry.

The problem isn't the consumption of information. The problem is the lack of action.

We have been given a treasure trove of tools. We must now learn to wield them.

We have been given an axe and taught how to use it. Now let us chop some wood.

We have been given a paintbrush and taught how to paint. Now let us make a masterpiece.

It is time for the student to become the master.

NOTE:

Throughout the book I will be referencing episodes from my show. If you would like to listen to a specific episode you can either go to www.DanielGefen.com/(episodenumber) for example to listen to episode 100 you would go to www.DanielGefen.com/100 or you could search for 'Can I Pick Your Brain?' on iTunes or any other podcasting app and find the episode.

My Story

School Can Be Cruel

Last night, I told my kids a bedtime story about a little boy who was the new kid in school.

He was introduced to the class and told to take a seat. But when he looked around the classroom, he saw that all the boys had placed their bag on the seat next to them.

They didn't want this new kid sitting next to them.

What if the new kid was weird?

What if he smelled bad?

What if he was a nerd?

What will everyone else think of me if I let him sit next to me?

As the new kid stood there, looking around for an empty chair, it seemed like an endless amount of time, filled with immense shame, sadness, and fear.

Suddenly, at the back of the room, a brave boy removed the bag from the chair next to him.

The new boy breathed a sigh of relief as he sat in the chair.

He became eternally grateful to that boy who had the heart and courage to accept him and welcome him into his space.

I turned to my children and said:

"You be the one that removes your bag from the chair next to you!"

Never let another human suffer because you are afraid of what others may think of you. We are all created to love each other, even though we may be different.

"But daddy was that a true story?"

"Yes. That new boy was me."

Who Am I?

So who is Daniel Gefen? It depends on whom you ask...

If you ask my parents, siblings, wife, children, friends, enemies (hopefully I don't have many), neighbors, members of my community, ex-school teachers, ex-classmates, business partners, clients, friends on social media, mentors and others I have interacted with in my life they will probably all tell you something different.

The truth is, it doesn't matter who they think I am.

Because what they think about me has nothing to do with me.

The reason why you will get a different answer depending on whom you ask is that each person sees me through their individual lenses. They will judge me based on their personal beliefs, experiences, self-image, upbringing, levels of security, and other unique characteristics. They will see me as a reflection of themselves. They will like the parts of me that they relate to and understand, and feel uncomfortable by the parts of themselves they don't understand.

You see, the biggest problem Self-help Addicts have is that we care too much about what people think of us. This is the root of the addiction.

Taking action without fear of what others will think is the cure for Self-help Addiction.

What other people think of you has nothing to do with you.

So who is Daniel Gefen?

I am who I think I am.

That's the power of my mind. *I get to create who I am.*

Every single moment of every single day I get to recreate myself.

I choose who I want to be based on my own thoughts, speech, and actions.

It's super powerful. So don't give away that power to others.

What you think of me has nothing to do with me.

I didn't always think that way. In fact, I have struggled all my life comparing myself to others, craving attention, trying to prove my self-worth, beating myself up inside, wearing the mask I thought you wanted to see.

I was the class clown. Desperately trying to get attention at any cost. I spent a lot of time in the headmaster's office.

When I was in high school, I was picked on. I was bullied emotionally, and I was called countless names including "Spider Face" (because of a mole on my cheek with hair growing out of it, which I later got frozen off), "Bugs Bunny" (my teeth stuck out a mile), and "dumb and stupid" because I was kept back a grade. (There was no room for me in the grade above.)

I had just one friend growing up and spent most of my youth sitting in his room playing video games, escaping from the pains of growing up.

I was raised in an Orthodox Jewish community in London called Stamford Hill. My father ran two kosher grocery stores where I sometimes helped out at busy times. He also did photography as a hobby and as a side gig. I would joke that I had 4 siblings. My brothers Yoel and Benjy, my sister Bracha, and the baby Canon. (The camera was attached to my dad like it was his baby). I was the oldest.

My mother was a stay at home mom. What can I say about my mom?

We got into our fights but I love her dearly and she means the world to me. (You know that, right? ;))

My first job was volunteering in a home for the mentally handicapped. That was a life awakening. You don't know how fortunate you are until you spend time with people who don't have the basic functionalities we take for granted.

Things like eating, going to the bathroom, driving a car, finding a soulmate, having children...life's simple pleasures are an unbreachable challenge for them.

Tricking my Wife into Marrying Me

When I met Lorren for the first time it was love at first sight ... at least for me . She was beautiful (and still is after having four kids). We met in Israel on vacation (interestingly, we now live here). She was from California and I was from England — two opposite ends of the world (physically and culturally).

I charmed her. I did all the usual, but she was playing hard to get. So I got on a plane. I literally had to chase her. Bear in mind, I'm an English boy who has never been to America, and here I am getting on a plane to go see her.

I had no idea where I was going to stay or what I was going to do. I literally just called up a couple of my friends.

"Hey, do you know anybody in California?"

They're like, "California is pretty big. Where in California?"

I'm like, "I think she lives in Los Angeles."

"Oh, yeah. I know a few friends."

I ended up crashing random people's houses until they kicked me out.

At one point, I really wanted to get engaged, and we had this weird conversation where I basically said to her, "Why are you not ready?"

She said to me, "I don't even know what it is. I think you're amazing. I really like you. I don't know. I love being with you, and I love just hanging with you. I think you're amazing and I think you'd be an amazing husband and an amazing father and everything, but I just don't know what it is."

I tried to dig a bit deeper. "Okay. well, can you try and think, maybe, what it could be?"

Then she says, "Okay, this is going to sound really weird, but I'm going to say it...

You're too nice."

I said, "What? What the heck do you mean? What do you mean I'm too nice? I thought that's a good thing?"

"It is, but I don't know. I just feel like you're just too nice."

"All right. What do you want me to do? Punch you in the face?"

I didn't know quite what to do.

So ... I played a little trick on her.

It's called reverse psychology.

Over the weekend she spent time with her friends and I spent time alone. I had time to think. Then it came to me. I knew what I needed to do, but it was going to be very risky.

I decided that it was the only way, as scary as it was.

I didn't call her. I waited for her to call me. Finally, she calls me up.

She says, "Hey, Daniel. How you doing?"

"Yeah, I'm good."

"How was your weekend?"

"Yeah, it was good. How was yours?"

"Yeah, I had a really good time with my friends."

Then I went for it.

"Listen, Lorren. I don't know how to say this buuuut I feel like there's no point dating anymore."

As I'm saying this, my heart is beating a thousand miles an hour.

She says "What? What do you mean? What are you saying?"

I said, "I don't know if it's going to go anywhere. Every time I go out with you, I fall more in love with you. And I just feel like I'm going to end up more broken. I feel like it's best that we just part ways and we just move on. I'll just go back to London and we'll go our separate ways."

My heart is racing like a Formula One race car as I'm saying this.

What if she calls my bluff?

Then she goes, "No, no. Let's go out one more time. Let's do one more date and then let's just see what happens. After that, you can decide but let's just go out one more time."

I said, "Okay. Fine but only if we play a game." (part 2 of my devious plan)

She says, "What game?"

I said, "I want to go to the beach and I want to play a game. It's called spin the bottle."

"You want to play spin the bottle?"

"Yes but here's the thing. Are you ready? These are the rules. I made up this game. It's called spin the bottle but you don't kiss."

"What?"

I said, "We will both write down 10 questions each but they have to be really deep questions, life-changing questions, everything that you want in your life. Questions like how you want to raise your children, what goals you want to achieve, what your biggest dreams and aspirations are, what you want to be written on your tombstone ... I want both of us to write down 10 of those really hard questions and then we're going to put them in a hat and we're going to spin the bottle. Whoever the bottle points to has to answer the question."

And that's what we did. We went to the beach, a little picnic, got the hat out. We started writing. We were really thinking hard about what questions we wanted to ask. We put them in the hat. We spun the bottle.

At the end of the game, Lorren looks me in the eye, smiles and says "I'm ready."

Living the High Life

The three key ingredients here were *Persistency, Creativity, and Courage.*

I didn't take no for an answer. I tapped into my creative mind to think of a way forward. I had the courage to take the action needed.

Today, I'm proud to say that it paid off big time. Through ups and downs, we have been happily married now for over 10 years and I can't imagine not having her by my side.

When I was 23, I managed to negotiate a six-figure salary position in Los Angeles. Life was great. I was married to the girl of my dreams, father to a precious little boy, living in a beautiful Spanish townhouse, driving a brand new car, and working on the 14th floor on Wilshire Boulevard overlooking the Hollywood sign.

Life couldn't be better.

Then 2008 came and hit me upside the head.

I got laid off. Was forced to take a commission-only sales position at a mortgage broker.

In 2008 you couldn't give away a mortgage for free!

I worked 16 hour days pounding the phones and after four months of not making a dime, I was completely broke.

Then the knock came at the door. That knock would change my life forever.

It was Olga the Russian landlady. She stood there towering over me with a very serious look on her face (not that she ever smiled)

"Mr. Gefen..." she said in her strong Russian accent "You need to pack up your things and leave"

I couldn't believe I was actually getting thrown out of my home.

"But I have a wife and a child..." I started to plead.

"Not my problem," came her cold response. "You haven't paid the rent in over two months."

I was shocked. I couldn't believe this was happening.

The next few months were a blur.

We moved into my in-law's home and I fell into a depression.

I felt so *powerless, helpless and useless.*

Things got so bad I ran away. I left my wife and child and crashed at a friend's house.

I was too ashamed and humiliated to face my family.

After a week, my friend told me I should go back. He told me that I would regret it if I didn't.

He said that I would lose the most precious things in my life.

He was right.

I called my wife but she didn't want to speak to me. She was too hurt and scared. What if I left her again? She wasn't sure she wanted me back.

My heart broke into a thousand pieces. I felt so broken. But something inside me told me I needed to fight for another chance and not give up. I begged her to give me a chance. I told her that I would do everything in my power to make things right.

I called up my father in England and it was one of the toughest phone calls I have ever had to make.

I had made him proud. I had married a beautiful girl from LA, made him a grandfather, and lived a luxurious lifestyle. But now here I was about to tell him that I was losing everything.

It hurt like hell. But I needed to do it.

Emotional Healing

My relationship with my father growing up wasn't easy.

He had grown up being emotionally and physically abused. His mother drowned in a lake when he was 14. His father was a Holocaust survivor. He showed his love by giving me whatever I wanted. He worked hard to provide for me and my three siblings. He never said " no" whenever I would ask for something. But he was emotionally crippled. He didn't know how to connect with me on an emotional level. I craved it.

Later on in life, we started to have deeper conversations and one time I built up the courage to say to him that all I ever wanted was for him to call me up randomly just to tell me he loved me.

He told me that it was hard for him to express himself and I told him that I understood, but that I believed he could do it when the time was right.

A few days later I was playing tennis. It was a Friday morning and my phone rang.

It was my father. I was surprised because my father never called me unless there was an emergency. I quickly picked up the phone hoping there wasn't any bad news.

"Hi, is everything ok?" I said

"I love you."

I nearly dropped the phone.

He did it. I told him how proud I was of him and how much I love him.

I will remember that moment for the rest of my life.

So there I was making a call to my father to let him know that I 'failed'.

I explained how I went broke and nearly got divorced. My ego melted away and I told him I needed help.

Without hesitation, he told me he would give me a job at his grocery store in England.

If you told me six months earlier that I would be moving back to England, working at the cashier in my father's grocery store, I would have told you that you were losing your mind. It was the last thing I would ever imagine happening. Life is funny that way.

When I told my wife we were moving to England she was hesitant. How could she move away from her parents with a man who recently ran away, leaving her alone? Could she trust me and go to a foreign country where she knew nobody?

Her heart and mind battled it out. Her heart won.

Not a day goes by that I don't appreciate my wife for sticking with me through everything.

Without her, I wouldn't have accomplished half of what I have. Without her, this book wouldn't have been written.

Starting Over

We landed in London with nothing other than 2 suitcases. We were starting over from scratch.

I hated working in my father's grocery store. I would stare at the clock waiting for the time to end each day. It was painful but it paid the bills, and for that, I am eternally grateful to him. It wasn't easy going from a 6 figure salary and living the luxury life to sitting in a grocery store all day, but I was happy that I was able to provide for my family.

After about a year I couldn't take it anymore. My inner entrepreneurial spirit was suffocating.

I needed to express the inner artist in me and it was being suppressed every day I was working for someone else. I wasn't using my gifts and talents. It was killing me.

I went home to my wife one day and broke down to her. "If I have to serve milk and eggs to one more person, I think I'm going to shoot someone."

She told me that she believed in me and that she would support me whatever I decide to do.

I called my father and told him that I was really grateful that he gave me a job but I wanted to start my own business. He was very supportive.

That day I felt a freedom like never before.

It was like walking out of a jail cell. My creativity was imprisoned and I had finally let it free.

My head was buzzing with ideas. So I went to a business advisor, a guy by the name of Shraga Zaltzman, who sat with me to go over some of those ideas.

Eventually, he told me of an idea he had that he thought would be perfect considering most companies were trying to cut down on costs. The idea was a call answering service. Instead of having to hire full-time receptionists, companies could transfer their calls to an answering service. This way they would save money (by only paying when calls were answered), handle multiple incoming calls at the same time and they wouldn't have to worry about sick days, lunch times, holidays, busy periods or hiring and firing staff. It was a perfect solution.

Jet Virtual was born.

Good is good enough

When I started the company I remember spending an insane amount of time trying to come up with the 'perfect' name. I must have written down over a hundred possible names.

Self-help Addicts tend to be perfectionists. We need everything to be perfect.

The logo needs to look perfect, the branding, the website, the brochures … these things are not what puts money in your bank account.

Nobody buys based on a logo or a name.

When was the last time you decided not to buy a product or service because you didn't like the name or the logo wasn't pretty enough?

I must have wasted my first precious months trying to get it all just right.

Anything to avoid actually picking up the phone and calling my first prospect.

Perfectionism is a great defense mechanism we use when we're scared to take action.

This book could have been published a long time ago had I not tried to make it 'perfect'.

The only reason you have this book in your hands right now is because I let go of my need for it to be perfect and just hit the publish button.

At the beginning, I was the sales guy, marketer, bookkeeper, receptionist, customer service rep, debt collector and CEO. It was tough, but it's the price you pay for the journey to freedom.

Interestingly, I may never have tasted real freedom if it wasn't for a devastating event that almost crippled my business.

Two years into building up Jet Virtual, I had an office filled with staff answering calls for hundreds of companies.

One of my weaknesses is managing people. I'm a visionary, not a manager.

I prefer to orchestrate rather than play the instruments.

I like to play in the clouds and not so much in the dirt (if that makes sense).

So I hired a manager, her name was Stacey, who took over operations. Hiring and firing staff, dealing with clients, chasing debts and making sure everything ran like clockwork — all the things I suck at.

It was still hard work and I found myself working more "in" my business than "on" it but that was about to change.

My 'AHA' Moment

One day I get a call. It was Stacey. She said she was sorry but she couldn't come into work.

I said "Oh, is everything OK? Will you be coming in tomorrow?"

There was a long silence and then she said "No, I can't come to work anymore. I almost committed suicide and my therapist said I can't go back to work."

I was stunned.

It was a massive shock and I completely didn't see it coming.

I relied on Stacey so much that I forgot how to operate my business.

I received another call that very same day. It was the office landlord telling me that we needed to vacate the office as they had sold the building.

Two heavy blows in one day. How was I going to find a replacement for Stacey with such short notice? Who was going to train them? Who was going to manage everything in the interim? How was I going to find a new office in the next three weeks? How are we going to answer calls for hundreds of companies while the equipment is moved over?

The pressure got too much; I left the office and ran home.

I went to my bedroom and sat on my bed like a little boy that broke his toy.

Negative thoughts plagued my mind. How will I get through this?

I picked up the phone and called my business mentor at the time. His name was Gavin Ucko.

I spent around 15 minutes venting. Dumping all my negativity onto him.

He just listened and heard me out.

Then he said, "Daniel, have you finished?"

I said "Yeah"

"Okay, now get off your self-pitying backside and go DO SOMETHING about it!"

I was shocked.

No sympathy. Just a big slap in the face - a much-needed slap in the face.

"You put your blood, sweat, and tears into this business, and you're not going to give it up without a fight. Now go use your creative mind to think of a solution. You're an entrepreneur, so act like one!"

His words penetrated deep and compelled me to action. I jumped off my bed, thanked him and went for a walk.

During that walk, I thought of all the possible solutions I could come up with.

Then an idea came to my mind. It was a crazy idea. So crazy that most people would have talked me out of it. But this one crazy idea radically changed my life and business career.

The idea was to *outsource my entire business to a competitor.*

That way I wouldn't have to worry about managing staff, equipment, clients, offices … and I can focus entirely on business growth activities.

The first thing I did was called up all my competitors and arranged to meet them to see if they were the right fit.

I was looking for a company I could trust to service my clients, and I needed to be able to negotiate a deal that made sense to me. I needed the margins to be large enough that I can make a good profit.

After meeting a few companies, I finally found the perfect match. I structured the deal so I would still retain ownership of all present and future clients and negotiated very good margins, which freed me to focus 100% on business development.

I remember reading a book called the E-Myth by Michael Gerber where he spoke about the importance of working ON your business instead of IN your business. Now for the first time, I was finally able to do just that. (I have recently had the honor of sharing a speaking stage with him.)

After going over all the fine details, shaking hands and signing the agreement, I walked out of the office and felt the taste of freedom once again.

Working from a Hotel Lobby

I fired my staff, sold the equipment and drove to a local hotel with just a laptop and a phone.

I ran and grew my entire company from that hotel lobby.

Every day I would park my car outside the hotel, and then pace the lobby closing deals on my phone all day long.

Over time, staff members would come up to me, thinking I was the hotel manager, and ask if they could take their lunch breaks. I would reply that I didn't mind when they took their lunch break, but I wasn't the manager.

This lasted a full year until one day I get a tap on the shoulder. It was the hotel manager.

"Excuse me, but can we have a word?" He asked in his super-posh British accent.

I said "sure," knowing that my time was up at the hotel.

He asked me if I lived at the hotel.

I laughed and said that I had a house with three children and a wife in it.

"So what, may I ask, are you doing here every day?"

"I am running my company from here."

He almost fell off his chair then asked me in the nicest possible way if I minded running my company from somewhere else.

I thanked him for the hospitality and left.

Outsourcing my company was the best thing I ever did.

Being "officeless" was so much fun and I felt so free. I was finally able to really focus on my core strengths, which I would discover later on while hosting a podcast show, writing a book, and building a following online.

I remember one time deciding to work in the local park. It was a sunny day and I thought, why not sit on a bench and work under a tree. As I was walking through the grass in the park to find the right bench someone was running towards me clutching a briefcase. I recognized him. He was in my class in high school.

"Where are you running to?" I asked him

"I'm running to catch the train to work," he replied and then asked, "Where are you going?"

I smiled and casually said, "Nowhere. I'm working from here."

He did a double take and looked surprised but didn't have time to slow down.

He was running to a packed train to take him to a busy office in the city.

I was chilling in the park enjoying the sun's rays, pretty flowers, and birds singing.

In school, I was considered the "reject." I was the class clown. I was told I would amount to nothing. I was laughed at. Now I got to have the last laugh.

Early Retirement

My dream was always to move to Israel. My plan was to retire there eventually.

One day, I decided to retire early. So at the age of thirty-one, I packed up my things, took my family and retired to live in Israel.

Retirement lasted only a few months. I got bored of playing tennis all day.

A guy by the name of Nachum Kligman called me up and asked me if I wanted to be a guest on his podcast show.

"A pod-what?" I asked. (It sounded like some sort of spaceship to me.)

"A podcast. It's like a radio show, but it's online. Kinda like what Netflix is to TV."

"Wow, that sounds awesome," I said. It sounded really exciting to me. I was never a guest on anything before. (Except maybe at someone's house or restaurant.)

I went on his show and fell in love. Not with him. (Though I do really love you Nachum ;))

I fell in love with speaking into a mic. I loved speaking, and I could speak for hours. Literally.

I couldn't believe that I was able to share my story with thousands of people at one time.

I fell in love with being on a platform and performing. I came to realize that I was a great performer. I always was. But it usually got me in trouble in school and at home. Now I could perform and it could impact other people's lives.

I fell in love with inspiring other people.

At the end of the show, I asked Nachum how I could start my own podcast show.

He agreed to help me and show me everything there was to know (for a small fee, of course :))

Can I Pick Your Brain?

After just two weeks I had my logo, name (*Can I Pick Your Brain?*), website (www.DanielGefen.com) equipment, and my first episode published.

I remember recording that first episode. I was soooo nervous! I recorded it 16 times because each time I messed up. Finally, I just hit the publish button. It was like taking that step out of the airplane while 15,000 feet in the air.

At the time of this writing, I have interviewed over 100 guests, reached over 150,000 downloads, and been rated in the top 26 business podcasts to listen to by CIO magazine as well as ranked in the top 50 on iTunes.

This is after launching the show only a year and a half ago. Prior to which I had no experience hosting anything.

I have also since been a guest on over 50 podcast shows.

After several months of producing episodes, my show started to get popular and I started getting tons of email from people pitching themselves to be a guest on the show.

Nine out of ten got sent to junk.

After several months of getting pitched, I realized that there was a great business opportunity here. If there is so much demand for people trying to get on podcasts, why don't I start a podcast booking service? I could help pitch them to the hosts (after all, as a host I know what a good pitch looks like), prepare them for the shows (I know what a great guest sounds like) and help them turn listeners into followers.

I also started getting a lot of people asking me how to start their own podcast.

Gefen Media Group was born and is today the fastest growing podcast media branding agency.

I've come a long way from being the class clown.

Less Information

What Do You REALLY Want?

> *There are two great days in a person's life - the day we are born and the day we discover why.*
>
> - William Barclay

● ● ● ● ●

You can have all the tools at your disposal. You can have all the knowledge, connections and opportunities available to you. But if you don't know what you really want, *nothing will matter.*

So many people are running, jumping, climbing, and trying to reach for *something*.

But when you ask them "What do you REALLY want?" They stand stiff, looking perplexed.

Some people think they know what they want, but when they achieve their goal they realize it wasn't really what they were looking for. It didn't give them the satisfaction they thought it would bring.

Sometimes we can't know what we want until we go on a journey and discover it along the way.

So what do **YOU** really want?

As you read this book, I want you to think about that question. I want you to ask it to yourself over and over again because it's the most important question you can ask yourself.

Coming up with the answer is half the battle. The other half I will discuss in this book.

As much as I wish I could, I can't answer the question for you. Only you can discover the answer for yourself. There is no right or wrong answer but once you uncover what it is, you will be one of the rare few that has a clear mission and purpose in life.

It all starts with 'why?' and it all ends with 'why?'

Why do I *really* want to publish this book?

Is it because I want to help lots of people or is it because I want people to think I'm awesome?

Why did I *really* want to get married?

Is it because I wanted to give to someone and love them unconditionally or is it because I wanted to be loved and I wanted someone to give to me unconditionally?

Why do I *really* want to be wealthy?

Is it because I want to be able to give lots of charity and help millions of people or is it because I want others to think I'm a "somebody"? Is it because I want my father to be proud of me? Is it because I never want to worry about money ever again?

Why do I *really* want to go to the gym?

Is it because I want to be healthier and feel better about myself, or is it because I want other people to be more attracted to me and accept me?

It could be that the answer to all these questions is "both." I want to help people AND I want people to think I'm awesome.

The question is which of the two is motivating you *more*?

Remember, there is no wrong answer.

Never stop questioning your motivations.

When you discover what truly motivates you and *why* it motivates you then you will be on your way to breaking the addictive cycle. The desperate hunt for that missing piece of the puzzle will be finally over.

That endless hole that you feel inside of you is the question that is begging to be answered.

What do I **really** want?

Action Step: *Write down on a piece of paper what you really want to achieve in life.*

Play The Long Game

"Adopt the pace of nature: her secret is patience"

- Ralph Waldo Emerson

● ● ● ● ●

I am naturally lazy, but because I push myself to produce, you see me as an overachiever.

By nature, I am an introvert, but because I put on an act in public, you see me as an extrovert.

I have inner doubts and have suffered from very low self-esteem, but because I push myself to conquer my inner demons and wear a mask of bravado, you see me as confident and sometimes even cocky.

I break nature, but you only see the results.

If you looked inside you would see something entirely different.

I am the man you see today because I didn't accept the status quo.

Most successful people you know are not successful by nature, so don't excuse yourself from achieving greatness.

They fought for that greatness. They broke their nature. They battled their inner demons. They ripped their comfort zone to pieces.

Over ... and over ... again.

What emerged was the person you see today.

The battle happens inside. Nobody sees the process. Don't be fooled by the outer layers and results.

Recognize that every successful entrepreneur, artist, gold medalist, professional, or champion must constantly break their nature to become who they are.

So stop looking at the achievements of others and start breaking your own nature.

What holds people back from taking action?

This question bothered me for so long. I asked many people and almost all of them said "fear", "perfectionism" and "self-doubt", but I dug deeper and found the real reason most people don't take action.

Impatience.

We don't take action because we don't see results immediately.

It's why social media is so addictive. It's instant gratification. Likes, comments, and shares make us feel good because we get it instantly.

We have become an impatient generation. Impatience is what holds us back from making a huge impact.

Mastering the art of patience

I'm one of the most impatient guys I know. I'm the guy that spends the extra cash to get my Amazon product delivered the next day (or the same day).

I have driven an hour to pick up a product at a store instead of waiting a day or two for my local store to have it in stock. I need to see results immediately or I start getting discouraged. I had to work very hard to keep reminding myself that patience wins the game. Life is a marathon, not a sprint.

The people who wait it out always win in the end. I recently watched one of the most hyped up boxing matches in history. Conor Mcgregor vs Floyd Mayweather. It very much reminded me of the famous story of the tortoise and the hare. Conor was like the hare. Young, fresh and quick. Floyd was like the tortoise. Old, slow and patient.

The first six rounds looked promising for Conor and I thought he would win. But in the 10th round, he tired out and the more experienced Floyd seized the opportunity he had patiently anticipated. With just a few good shots to the head, Conor was out. Floyd had won. I see this all the time.

The ones who are patient and play the "long game" ultimately win. Self-help Addicts tend to be highly impatient. It's one of the main reasons we don't take action.

Building muscle at the gym takes time. Losing weight takes time. Running a marathon takes time. Building a successful business takes time. Creating deep, meaningful relationships take time.

Anything worthwhile takes time and consistency. And being able to consistently "show up" takes a lot of patience.

So how do we build our patience muscles?

For me, it helps to look at the big picture. Many times I find myself thinking about throwing in the towel because I am not seeing results. Usually, I just need to remind myself that everything I have ever done that is truly meaningful and impactful in my life has taken time.

Growing my first business to become profitable took over three years.

Getting my podcast show to over 100 episodes has taken almost two years.

Building a deep relationship with my wife has taken 10 years (and counting).

Writing this book has taken many years of thinking and almost a year of writing.

The daily grind can get discouraging if we forget the bigger picture.

But when we invest our time into something we reap the benefits in the long run.

My first business still pays all of my bills, and I don't work in the business anymore.

My podcast show has opened countless doors and relationships that are priceless.

My wife is my best friend and we will hopefully share many more happy years together.

My book will inspire countless people to take action and transform their lives for generations to come (even after I leave this world).

Stop wasting your time trying to cut corners and chasing the quick fixes.

Play the long game. Run the marathon. Win.

Action Step: *Practice telling yourself that worthwhile things take time.*

Take Full Control

"Only you can control your future"

- Dr. Seuss

● ● ● ● ●

There came a time in my life when I realized that nobody was going to give me a secret key or magical pill.

It didn't exist.

If I wanted to become a great speaker and bestselling author I was going to have to speak and write over and over again.

If I wanted to make a lot of money I was going to have to work hard, think creatively, and leverage every resource I had available to me.

I realized that nobody cared about my success more than I did.

*Many people can show you the door but only **you** can walk through it.*

Some people prefer to give up control because they don't trust themselves to be able to make the right choices. Sometimes we prefer to give someone else control so we don't have to take the blame if things go wrong.

Here's a little secret.

If you want to be successful in anything you do, you must take full control.

Nobody cares about your success as much as you, and nobody will ever create success for you.

No self-proclaiming life guru is going to get you in shape, put more money in your bank account, or save your marriage.

You are the captain of your ship. You choose to steer it where you want.

Only you can take the necessary steps to reaching your destination.

There came a time in my life when I had to stop searching for my hero. I had to *become my hero.*

I started telling myself over and over again:

"I am in control, and I will trust my own decisions. I will take full responsibility if things go wrong, and full credit if things go well. I will not be afraid to fail because I will learn from my mistakes and try again with the extra knowledge and experience gained. I will succeed without needing permission from others.

I am the captain of my ship."

I started my first business because I didn't want to work for someone else. It was tough because I was giving up a steady job and I had a wife and two little boys to support at the time. I took the plunge because I felt that I was going to be miserable until I did. As difficult as it was, I am so happy I did. I felt free. I felt completely in control and although there were down times, overall it was an incredible experience and I built a successful business that I am proud of.

I take my lunch break when I get hungry.
I take a vacation when I feel like one.
I work in my boxers if I feel like it.
I am free to express my ideas.
I work with people I like.
I have unlimited earning potential.

I have endless amounts of opportunities.
I do what I like and delegate what I don't.
I take off time to spend with my family when I want.
I work from wherever in the world I choose to be.
I am the one to decide the value of my time.
I am building my own empire.
I am an entrepreneur.

From Powerless Alcoholic to Powerful Businesswoman

At one point, Tamara Thompson had only $4.00 to her name and was convicted several times for drunk driving.

In my interview with her (episode 58), she talked about how the turning point for her was when she took 100% responsibility for her life and turned it around.

Today she has more than seven years of sobriety and runs a hugely successful video production company called Serious Take Productions.

From Sleeping in a Restaurant to Owning 55 of Them

Greg Walker didn't speak until he was 11 years old.

He was told from a very young age that he was a "Big Dreamer" and was told to drop out of school because he didn't have a chance at success.

Both his parents were alcoholics and all his siblings ended up in jail.

The Self Help Addict

Greg told me that he remembers the day when his father held a gun to his sister's head. He felt completely powerless.

But he was determined to make a change in his life. He was going to be different. He was going to take responsibility for his own life.

He ended up working in a local restaurant cleaning the floors and would often sleep there to avoid going home.

Eventually, he was promoted to manage the restaurant and one day the owners offered to sell it to him as they wished to retire.

This "Big Dreamer" went on to owning fifty-five restaurants and becoming a self-made millionaire.

Remember that *you are the captain of your ship.*

Action Step: *Pick one thing in your life that you feel you are losing control over and start gaining back control*

Go From Consumer To Creator

"The way to get started is to quit talking and begin doing."

- Walt Disney

● ● ● ● ●

Let me ask you a few questions.

How many books have you read in your life? *How many have you written?*

How many speeches have you listened to? *How many have you given?*

How many videos have you watched? *How many have you produced?*

How many seminars have you been to? *How many have you run?*

How many quotes have you been inspired by? *How many of your quotes have inspired others?*

As a self-help addict, I read tons of self-help books, watched hundreds of videos, listened to many lectures and attended dozens of seminars.

One day I asked myself one question.

After consuming all this information *how much have I produced?*

This one question led me to start my own podcast show and produce over 100 episodes where I interviewed some of the most successful entrepreneurs in the world.

This one question led me to launch and grow multiple successful businesses.

This one question led me to start consulting other business owners.

This one question led me to speak in front of thousands of people.

This one question led me to write the book you are holding in your hands.

This one question helped me go from a consumer to a creator.

The difference between you and someone like Tony Robbins, Steve Jobs, or Oprah Winfrey is that they are creators. They are constantly producing.

Being a creator is scary. It requires hard work. Comparatively, being a consumer is safe and easy.

Anyone who has been massively successful started by producing something small. They took one step. They were most likely scared. Maybe petrified. But they took that first step and after a while, they looked back at everything they had produced and were astounded.

That is the power of momentum.

When we take consistent action over time, we get MASSIVE results.

You can become a creator today.

Just write the first page of your book.

Record your first audio of your podcast show.

Do your first Facebook live video.

Take your first guitar lesson.

Take that first step.

A Lesson From a Billionaire

I had the honor of having a billionaire on my show. (Episode 102)

Jeff Hoffman has been part of a number of well-known companies, including Priceline.com, Booking.com, uBid.com, ColorJar, among others. He also serves on the boards of companies across the globe, supporting entrepreneurs and small businesses in more than 150 countries. He also supports the White House, the US State Department, the United Nations, and foreign governments on economic growth initiatives and entrepreneurship.

While I was preparing for the episode I kept asking myself, "What should I ask a Billionaire?!"

There are only 2000 Billionaires in the world, so this was a huge opportunity.

I wanted to know what it took to become one of the wealthiest people on the planet.

Was it luck? Connections? Skill? IQ? Was it raw determination and passion?

Or was it something else entirely?

When I asked Jeff the question, he said that he has a sign up in his office that says,

"Ideas are welcome here but execution is worshiped"

Converting Inspiration Into Action

I have a rule: for every chapter I read or any material I consume, I must produce something.

It could be a blog post or a chapter in my book. When I hear a good quote, I make it into an article or post on social media. I want to train myself to *convert inspiration into action.*

We get inspired but soon enough, the inspiration fades. The secret to ensuring that inspiration doesn't become just another superficial "high" is to act on it. Make it real. Make it tangible.

I have lost count of how many times I have been incredibly inspired by something but did nothing about it. A movie inspired me to tell my dad "I love you", but the feeling left me within the hour.

The opportunity passed me by.

Action is best taken in the "heat" of the moment. If we wait too long, we cool down.

Seize those moments. Make big things happen while you're still inspired to act.

Train yourself to *convert feelings into concrete actions.*

100,000 Burpees

Joshua Spodek is one of the most accomplished people I've ever met.

When I researched him for my show (episode 108), I couldn't believe his list of accomplishments.

He holds five Ivy-League degrees, including a PhD in Astrophysics and an MBA from Columbia University. He has finished six marathons, holds six patents, and has co-founded several education ventures. He has competed at the World and National level of Ultimate Frisbee, including playing at the first Ultimate Tournament in North Korea (yeah, *North Korea*!), swam across the Hudson River, has done over 100,000 burpees (Google it), wrote over 2,700 blog posts, has jumped out of two airplanes, and has visited 26 countries on six continents.

If that's not enough, he helped build an X-ray observational satellite orbiting the Earth as part of a multi-billion-dollar decade-plus mission led by the European Space Agency with NASA!

Taking advantage of being one of few people in the world to have visited North Korea twice, he has lectured and published a book on North Korean war strategy.

His work as an artist has won him an Obie Award for Design Excellence and reached the semifinals in the Adobe Design Achievement Awards.

He's also the author of the bestselling book *'Leadership Step by Step'*.

What's his secret?

One word. *Consistency.*

Joshua claims that his consistency has helped him achieve more than any other factor.

It's never too late

I decided to get braces at the age of 32 while married with four children.

I started learning piano at 30.

I developed a relationship with my father in his 50's.

I started a podcast show with no previous speaking experience. I decided to write a book after 10 years of dawdling and anticipation.

It's never too late to make big changes in your life.

Start Putting Yourself Out There

When I interviewed Russell Brunson (Episode 79), he shared a crazy story about one of his clients who posted a Facebook Live video every day without any traction. She felt like she was speaking to a black hole.

Then one day something unexpected happened.

While recording her daily Facebook Live video, she got really nervous and peed her pants.

She was so embarrassed and thankful that not too many people were watching. Well. That video got shared. Then it got shared some more. Then it went viral.

It reached more than five million views!

Within 12 months, she made more than a million dollars in coaching fees!

Here's the lesson: You never know when your video, blog post, podcast episode, or image will go viral. It may just be at your most raw moment. In fact, it usually happens when you least expect it.

The secret is to keep putting yourself out there. Keep posting content. Keep showing up.

The most successful people are the ones that consistently produce. Stop thinking about what people will think. One day you will look back and say "Wow, I'm so glad I stuck with it!"

Here's a little challenge: Record a Facebook Live video every day this week.

It shouldn't be longer than three minutes and talk about anything you like. You can even talk about how scared you are to post a Facebook Live video. Just get into the habit of producing content. It will improve your self-confidence, sharpen your communication skills and lower the volume of that annoying perfectionist inside your head.

Go make it happen.

Action Step: *Start getting into a habit of producing something for everything you consume*

Think Less, Do More

"Small deeds done are better than great deeds planned."

— Peter Marshall

● ● ● ● ●

If I had thought long enough about most of the important choices I have made in my life, I wouldn't have made them.

As Self-help Addicts we tend to get stuck inside our own heads. Overthinking and overanalyzing things. We are great at finding reasons not to take action. We are masters at putting things off. Perfectionist is a nicer way of saying first-class procrastinator.

Our excuse for avoiding most things is that we need to wait for the right time or the right opportunity.

If I would have allowed myself to think enough about starting a podcast show, I would never have started one. It happened because I stopped *thinking* about doing it and *started doing it.*

Do you know how many times I talked myself out of writing this book? I have lost count.

This book would have never been published if I didn't force myself to stop thinking and just start typing.

The problem is *we are too smart for our own good.*

We think we will take better action if we think about it more.

The truth is that *the more we think the better we become at thinking. The more we take action the better we become at taking action.*

You become a better basketball player by throwing more balls. You become a better writer by writing more. You become a better speaker by speaking more.

It's not the thinking that makes us better performers. It's the performing.

I'm a better podcast host because I have produced more podcast shows. I'm a better businessman because I have more experience running businesses. Reading books on being a better parent or spouse is fine, but I'm a better father because I spend more time with my kids. I'm a better husband because I spend more time with my wife. Sometimes we complicate things so we don't have to deal with them.

Make Quick Decisions

Making quick decisions is key to successfully reaching goals and in order to make quick decisions, you need to trust yourself.

Like building trust with others you also need to build trust with yourself. You need to earn your own trust. You can get to the point where because you trust yourself so much you also value yourself more. You are not afraid to make your own decisions anymore. You can take action without researching the heck out of something. You stop doubting your own judgments.

So how do you build trust?

You need to make a decision and go with it. Don't think about it; just do it. It's as simple as that. You will be surprised at how liberated you will feel just doing this for the first time.

I used to take ages picking out a shampoo bottle in the supermarket. I would sniff each brand, and go back and forth between them deciding the RIGHT one to buy.

The first time I walked into a store, picked up the first bottle of shampoo, and put it in my basket without stopping felt great. I know this seems crazy but these little things are so important in the bigger picture.

Just like when you go to the gym you need to start with light weights and then work up to the heavier ones, so too you need to start making decisions with something small — like not spending too long picking out something to wear. These exercises of making quick decisions and not overthinking will train you to make quick decisions when necessary. It will stop you from wasting too much time overthinking when you could be getting more things done.

How many self-help books did your grandma read?

We read books and go to lecturers to learn how to do things instinctively known by our great, grandparents. My grandmother never read a book about raising children, and yet she managed to raise 10 children successfully. The truth is we also instinctively know, but we choose more education over hard work.

We live in a generation where more information is an escape from having to do the hard work.

We lack consistency because we live in a world of inconsistency. Technology has made us impatient, lazy and ungrateful. We expect to get something for little or no effort.

Every moment I spend consuming information I escape from having to produce something.

When I am thinking about doing something, I am channeling all my energy to thinking. When I am actively doing something, I am channeling my energy towards taking that action. Your energy can either be used for potential or for actual.

Do you want to spend your life being "potentially good" at something or actually good at something?

Do you talk the talk or walk the walk?

The only difference between talkers and walkers is where they choose to channel their energy. Talkers channel their energy to talking about stuff. Walkers channel their energy into getting stuff done.

Who would you prefer to hang out with? Who would you prefer to have on your team? Who would you prefer to hire?

Lazy Dad Syndrome

It was one of those days when I just didn't feel like doing anything. My body felt tired and I was in one of those trance-like slumps. It was the afternoon, and my kids came home from school asking to go to the park. My wife asked if I wanted to join, and I figured that I wasn't going to get any work done anyway so I might as well join them.

We got to the park and my two boys and little girl went running towards the slides and swings play area. I stood there and watched them play, still in my little slump. After a while, my wife nudged me and said, "Hey, why don't you go and join them? They love when their daddy plays."

"Nah, I'm not in the mood."

I stood there for a few more minutes and then slowly shuffled towards them. I noticed a pirate ship, which you rock back-and-forth on. "I'm really not in the mood," I said to myself.

My body felt heavy. I moved a little closer.

I slowly lifted myself onto the pirate ship making a grunting sound as if I had just lifted the back of a bus.

One of my boys noticed me get onto the pirate ship.

"Hey look, daddy is on the pirate ship," my seven-year old said to my eight-year old.

They quickly ran towards me as I started rocking the boat back and forth.

"Don't you dare come on my ship," I said in a rather lame pirate voice

They accepted my challenge and started to try and get onto the ship.

We wrestled. We ran. We laughed. They eventually threw me off into the deep ocean below.

The sun set and we drove back home.

This is one of many occasions when I just didn't feel like doing something, but I did it anyway. I have always been so thankful I did.

If You Take Action. The Feelings Will Follow.

People always say things like "I don't *feel* like going to the gym today"
"I don't *feel* like cleaning the house"
"I'm not *in the mood* to... "

Feelings are just feelings. I respect my feelings, and I recognize them. But I also know that they don't control me. They don't last. They only last as long as I want them to.
I can be angry for as long as I want to be angry. I can feel lazy as long as I want to feel lazy.

Many times before going to the gym I have that same feeling. "Oh man, I can't be bothered with this ."
But a strange thing happens once I actually get to the gym and start lifting weights.
I start to feel alive. I start to feel invigorated. Energized. Pumped.
When I leave the gym after a good workout I feel fantastic. I'm always glad I pushed myself to go.

It's the same thing when getting up in the morning. It feels good to roll over and go back to hibernating under my warm covers. It never feels good waking up late and having to be in a mad rush to get things done. When I push aside the morning feelings of sleep deprivation and get up anyway, within 10 minutes I feel fine. Within an hour I'm really glad I didn't sleep in.

Sometimes, I don't feel like saying sorry. It's uncomfortable. Especially when it's to my wife :)
But when I take the action and say sorry even though I don't feel like it, I always feel better about myself and know that I did the right thing.

Life is great when we set aside our negative feelings and take action even if it feels difficult.

Many times while writing this book I didn't feel like writing. I had to force myself to sit down and stare at my screen until my eyes glazed over. I wouldn't move from my seat until I had written something. Anything. And just like magic whenever I started writing my fingers would start to dance across the keyboard. Words turned into sentences. Sentences turned into paragraphs. Paragraphs turned into pages. Pages turned into the book (or Kindle) you hold in your hand.

It's no surprise that the number-one cure for depression is exercise.

There is something magical that happens when we simply move our body. Movement seems to wake up our positive emotions. It stimulates the parts of our brain that are switched off. Running boosts our brain power and helps our memory, among many other things.

If you have ever gone for a run you will know that your thinking becomes clearer. The world seems brighter, more colorful, and more vibrant. You get into a better mood and are more likely to smile and greet other people. Your body feels more open and free.

Creating Momentum

When we take action, we create momentum. Momentum is one of those powerful forces that when activated can make you unstoppable. You know what I'm talking about if you have ever been engaged in an activity for a prolonged period of time and at some point, you stop thinking.

Your body just moves with ease and you enter a state known as "flow" or what we call being in "the zone." You can achieve more than you can ever imagine if you can learn how to access this power more often.

The secret to creating momentum is simply taking continuous action.

Feel those feelings. Hear those negative thoughts.

Then say, *"I feel what you're feeling and I hear what you're saying but I'm doing it anyway!"*

Talk to your thoughts and feelings as if they are your little kids trying to get their way.

"Okay, Anger, I know you're angry and it's understandable, but you are not helping me right now."

"Hi, Fear, how are you doing? I hear what you're saying, but I know I can do this."

"Hey, depression I'm going for a run now, do you wanna join me?"

Remember: *Your thoughts and feelings are only as real as you make them.*

Action Steps: *Think of something you usually take a while to make a decision about and make a snap decision without changing your mind. Practice talking to your thoughts and feeling. Imagine them as your little children. They don't control you.*

Be Persistent

"If you are going through hell, keep going."

– Winston Churchill

● ● ● ● ●

Craving For Chocolate

When I was about four years old, my parents took me to a forest in England. It was in the middle of nowhere and I suddenly had the desire to eat some chocolate. I turned to my mother and said, "I want chocolate." She responded, "Oh, I'm really sorry, dear, but we didn't bring chocolate. I have some pretzels and some other snacks, if you like."

I said, "But, I want chocolate." And, she said, "Yeah, but we're in a forest. We're in the middle of nowhere and there's no chocolate." And, I said, "But I want chocolate."

She goes, "I know but ..." Then I went into this song that I created on the spot and it went like something like this…

"I want chocolate. I want chocolate. I want chocolate. I want chocolate. I want chocolate. I want chocolate. I want chocolate. I waaaaaaaaaant chocolate."

I went on and on and on for about an hour straight until my mother was literally going to pull her hair out and just have a complete nervous breakdown.

She finally grabs me by the hand and says, "All right. All right. Just stop singing that song. We'll get you chocolate. Let's go."

My father is busy taking pictures of the scenery and my mother says, "We've got to go. We've got to go. He needs to get his chocolate!"

We get into the car, and we drive around. We try to find a place. Finally, I got my chocolate.

There I am standing with a big grin on my face while I open up my chocolate bar and realize for the first time that I can get whatever I want if I didn't give in.

That was the persistent little brat inside of me.

I have been persistent (some may say a stubborn ass) ever since.

If you ask me, "What is the number one component to your success?" It is that I don't give up.

I just keep going.

You see, the thing I learned from an early age is that if you keep asking, pushing, questioning, trying, searching, and experimenting ... enough, you will eventually get what you want.

An Unexpected Call

When I started my first company I would cold call prospective clients and unless someone told me to jump in a cold lake, I would keep calling them every day.

One day, I called a gentleman by the name of Gary. I had probably called Gary four days in a row. This was day five. He was not happy. In fact, he gave me a twenty-minute lecture about how I was bordering on harassment and sounded desperate. At the end of the twenty-minute lecture, he surprised me and said he wished to sign up for my service!

That's not the end of the story.

About an hour after I put down the phone I received a call. It was Gary again.

Oh no, I thought, *he's probably going to cancel or give me another lecture.*

Another complete surprise. Gary told me that he was a venture capitalist who had recently sold his recruitment agency for £300 Million and that he really like my "style."

Gary wanted to invest in me.

We ended up having a meeting and he offered to buy 70% of my business, which I politely turned down.

This was yet another example of persistence paying off.

Even though it may rub certain people the wrong way, it pays to be persistent. The most successful entrepreneurs, athletes, scientists, and inventors are extremely persistent.

They are also patient. To be persistent, also requires having patience and a very thick skin.

Everyone falls.

The difference between self-help addicts and successful leaders is the difference between one who stays down and who gets back up.

Everyone makes mistakes. Super successful people learn from their mistakes and use the experience to get stronger. They see the mistake as a lesson learned rather than a failure.

Chutzpah

How do I get such incredible guests for my show?

How do I close deals worth 1,000's of dollars in a 20-minute phone call?

How do I get things done when so many people don't?

The answer is one word.

CHUTZPAH

I don't care about getting rejected. Rejection for me is part of the process.

What's the worst that can happen? They say "no" — big deal.

If you don't ask, you won't get. Simple.

Some might call it being a "risk taker."

I think the opposite.

NOT asking is being a "risk taker"

You risk every possibility and opportunity when you don't ask.

So *stop being a risk taker and develop some Chutzpah.*

The Man That Can Make (Almost) Anything Happen

Steve Sims is known as the real life Santa Clause. He is the magic genie that can make just about anything happen (for a small price).

Some of the things he has arranged for his clients have been:

A tour of the Titanic.

Playing alongside the Rolling Stones at a live concert.

Dinner with a favorite movie star.

Walking the runway at New York's Fashion week.

Getting married at the Vatican by the Pope himself!

He has even arranged for police to chase one of his clients through the streets of Monaco to reenact their favorite Bond movie scene!

So how does someone who started out as a simple bricklayer with no connections become the man that can make (almost) anything happen?

His answer to me was simple. You just ask. You practice asking over and over again. Because you have nothing to lose by asking and everything to gain.

Everything is Negotiable

Don't accept things as they are. Everything is negotiable. A hundred years ago nobody could believe that there would be airplanes taking people in the air. It was unimaginable that a person would get into a piece of metal and lift off the ground thousands of feet. Until the Wright brothers came along and proved to the world that it could be done. Nobody believed that.

Remember that nothing is set in stone. Everything is possible. Get in the habit of thinking "How can I do X?" instead of giving up and accepting defeat.

From Eating Out of Dumpsters to Making Millions

When I interviewed Bedros Keuilian (episode 47) I had tears in my eyes.

His father bribed the Russian government to escape communist Russia.

He describes how when he was a young boy his father would throw him into dumpsters to find something to bring home for dinner.

Most kids like that end up giving up on life and turn to substance abuse, gangs, and violence.

Bedros chose a different path. He built himself from the ground up.

In fact, he went from living in a truck and eating out of dumpsters to amassing millions in the fitness industry!

It wasn't easy, but he kept pushing forward and at one point even worked as a bouncer at a gay bar, but that's a story for another time.

Today, he is considered one of the most influential people in the fitness industry and has coached over 9,000 businesses!

Success is the difference between persistence and giving up.

The Power of *Just One More*

It's amazing how many times I tried just one more time and on *that* attempt, I succeeded.

I have gotten myself into a habit of always trying *just one more time* and it has worked wonders.

If I'm at the gym and I feel like getting off the treadmill, I tell myself "just one more minute."

If I'm emailing potential prospects for business, I will tell myself "send just one more email."

If I'm down 3 points in tennis I tell myself, "Just get one more point."

If someone tells me "no" I ask them *just one more time.*

It really works.

If Edison didn't try one more time, he wouldn't have invented the lightbulb.

If JK Rowling didn't ask one more publisher, you would never have heard of Harry Potter.

If Jim Carrey had quit after being booed off stage, he wouldn't have become one of the world's highest-paid actors and most famous comedians.

If Michael Jordan had given up after being cut from his high school basketball team, he wouldn't have become the greatest basketball player of all time.

As Billionaire owner of the NBA's Dallas Mavericks, Mark Cuban says,

"You only have to be right once."

Action Step: *Practice trying one more time. Make one more phone call. Hold on for one more minute. Run one more lap. Take one more chance.*

Make Fear Your Friend

Fear is at the deep routed core of all self-help addicts

– Daniel Gefen
(Yeah, I quoted myself :))

• • • • •

Doubt and indecision are the "helpers" of Fear. If doubt and indecision are the roots of fear then *clarity and decisiveness are the swords that cut through the roots of fear*. I was scared to run my own business.

I was scared to speak into a mic.

I was scared to get on stage.

I was scared to commit to one person.

I was scared to write a book.

And I'll let you in on a little secret: I'm still scared.

Even after doing more than 100 episodes, I still feel like throwing up every time I'm about to get on the mic! I'm still scared to publish this book. I'm still scared to get up on stage. I'm still scared that my businesses may fail. And yes, I'm still scared my wife might leave me (okay, maybe not).

The point is that even though I feel the fear, I take action anyway. Because *the only cure for fear is to face it in the eye.*

I used to have a phobia of spiders. If I knew there was a spider somewhere in the house, I couldn't sleep.

This became a real problem once I got married.

My wife would yell about a big spider in the corner, and I told her to kill it herself.

She would say "I thought you were the man of the house?"

This obviously got me worked up. I AM the man of the house!

So I walked slowly over to the huge ginormous scary monster with a very large broom, and with my eyes closed, I smashed it five times to make sure it was really dead.

Then I left it, squashed on the wall.

There was no way I was going to touch it even with gloves.

The next time, I used my shoe.

Then I started feeling a little braver, so I removed it with a towel.

Eventually, I mustered up the courage, walked over, and with just a piece of tissue paper separating us, I pinched the spider while still alive, and took it out into the garden.

Today, spiders don't bother me.

The same is true for needles. I would shake uncontrollably out of fear whenever I had to get a shot.

Then one day, as I sat in the dentist chair and he was about to stick this needle the size of a hockey stick in my mouth, I closed my eyes and counted down from ten.

I told myself that the pain would only last ten seconds. If I could handle ten seconds of pain I was fine.

I am no longer terrified of needles.

Don't get me wrong, I don't go round pricking myself for fun. But I'm no longer paralyzed with fear by them.

Lessons from a UFC Fighter

I had the pleasure of picking the brain of former UFC fighter, CFFC Lightweight Champion, ROC Welterweight Champion, and VFL Welterweight Champion Charlie 'The Spaniard' Brenneman (episode 91).

Charlie left a full-time job as a Spanish teacher to pursue a career in mixed martial arts, which led him to a career as a UFC fighter and finding himself going head-to-head with the best fighters in the world. When I asked him how he felt walking towards the ring about to face his fierce opponent, he said that the adrenaline just took over. He would feel the fear and channel it to his advantage.

Fear is Your Friend

Your Fear will always be there to some degree. You can't get rid of it. In fact, you don't want to get rid of it. *Fear gives you an edge.* It increases your energy and gets your adrenaline pumping. If you didn't have fear, you would come across as boring and uninteresting. Fear keeps you humble and likable. Fear makes things exciting.

It's amazing how people react when I tell them I feel nervous or fearful about something. They usually sympathize, and are more likely to open up to me. *Fear gives us the gift of being vulnerable*. We tend to be more attracted to people who are genuine, open, vulnerable, and humble than people who are fake, closed, defensive, and arrogant.

So make fear your friend and not your enemy.

Give fear a big hug and say, "Hey, thanks for being such a good friend."

Action Step: *Write a list of all your fears. Then, one by one, try and face them. Talk to them. Become friends with them. Let yourself feel the fear and then take action to conquer your fear.*

The Paradox Of Choice

"Simplicity is the ultimate sophistication."

– Clare Boothe Luce

• • • • •

In today's world, we live in abundance. The internet has opened the doors for anyone to get into pretty much any industry.

The problem is that abundance can also lead to feeling overwhelmed.

Barry Schwartz wrote a groundbreaking book called "Paradox of choice" where he shows how too much choice leads to indecisiveness. He gives the example of an experiment where women were offered to buy a certain dress. One group was offered several colors to choose from, and the other group was only given a choice of two colors. Interestingly, the group that was offered only two choices decided quicker and was more likely to make a purchase. The other group took longer and usually ended up not buying because they felt overwhelmed.

Psychologists Sheena Iyengar and Mark Lepper published a remarkable study. On one day, shoppers at an upscale food market saw a display table with 24 varieties of gourmet jam. Those who sampled the spreads received a coupon for $1 off any jam. On another day, shoppers saw a similar table, except that only six varieties of the jam were on display. The large display attracted more interest than the small one. But when the time came to purchase, people who saw the large display were one-tenth as likely to buy as people who saw the small display.

Other studies have confirmed this result that *more choice is not always better.*

That's why so many people are struggling to make a living online.

You need to limit your options.

Self-help addicts tend to spend much of their time making decisions.

Should the logo be black or white?

Should I open up this type of bank account?

Which laptop should I buy?

Leaders make quick decisions and spend their time getting on with things.

Keep it Simple Silly

People over complicate things. Business, relationships, and life in general really can be made more simple, and usually, the more simple you keep it the more successful and enjoyable life becomes.

Take Apple and Google, for example. Apple decided to create a phone that had a simple design and simple user experience. Google's homepage was the most simple with just a search bar and nothing else. Both companies dominated their space because while their competitors were trying to do *more* they did *less.*

Their focus on simplicity is what made them the undisputed champions of their industries

Homeless to Millionaire

One of the most shocking interviews I did was with Dawnna St Louis (Episode 81).

I was sitting on the edge of my chair when Dawnna shared her crazy story of how she went from homeless and living in her car for six months to building and selling her tech consultancy firm for a quarter of a billion dollars!

She talked about how she would wash the windows of a local gym in exchange for a shower and a cereal bar. That's all she survived on during her darkest days.

When I asked her what she thought was the biggest factor for going from such a low place to becoming a self-made millionaire she said *"I kept it simple."*

She had nothing to lose and very few options were available to her. No money, no connections, and very few resources meant less time to think, and more time to just *take simple action.*

One simple action after another led her to go from living out of her car to living out her dreams.

If you limit your decisions and keep things really simple, you too will find that you will get a lot more done and won't waste time making choices or overthinking things.

Positioning your sticks

The story goes that there was once a farmer riding his donkey in the desert, and he came across a "homeless" man crawling on the ground dying of thirst. He quickly jumped off and loaded him onto his donkey. He gave him something to drink and took him back to his home to give him some food.

The stranger gobbled down some bread and soup and was so exhausted he fell asleep at the table.

The farmer carried his guest into the barn and lay him down on the hay where he slept for almost two full days.

Upon awakening, the "homeless" man called out to the farmer.

The farmer hurried into the barn, asking if his guest was feeling well and if he would like something to eat and drink.

"I am feeling much better thanks to you," he said.

"This may come as a surprise, but I am not a homeless beggar. I am the king, and I was robbed and kidnapped by bandits and left in the desert to die. My people have probably been wondering where I have gone so I must be on my way, but you have saved my life - for which I am eternally grateful and will repay you handsomely. As you saved me from the lifeless desert, I will fill the desert with as much gold as you desire. Place four sticks into the sand and between those four posts gold shall be deposited as my gift to you."

The farmer almost fainted from shock. He couldn't believe his luck.

He wasted no time and grabbed four sticks to go and claim his fortune.

He placed one stick in the sand and started walking knowing that the greater the distance between each stick, the greater the amount of gold would be his.

Each time he was about to place the second stick into the sand he stopped and said to himself "Why not go a little further and become even more wealthy."

And so he kept walking. And walking. And walking.

Legend has it that he's still walking until this very day.

Don't get stuck in the desert

Self-help Addicts keep "walking."

Waiting for the bigger opportunity to present itself.

Our "desert" is huge and the possibilities are endless.

We tend to have very big eyes. *We want it all, and we want it all now.*

Perfectionism, impatience, and greed lead us to become overwhelmed and passive.

We let visions of grandiosity take over our minds, and we become complacent.

We idolize successful people, and ignorantly believe they experienced overnight success.

Our expectations become unrealistic and unachievable.

We feel inferior and less able, so we sabotage ourselves, and blame people and things out of our control to avoid taking any responsibility.

There is nothing wrong with having big goals, dreams, and aspirations.

But we must understand, if we don't put our sticks into the ground, we will end up empty handed.

When you try to grab too much, you end up grabbing nothin.

Action Step: *The next choice you confront, go with the simplest solution. Practice making quick decisions and being okay with whatever you decide. Remind yourself that you will learn more from failure than success and that time is your most precious asset.*

Commit Distraction Suicide

"We are surrounded by modern, time-saving devices, yet never seem to have enough time."

– Barry Schwartz

• • • • •

You know how your computer or phone slows down when there are too many tabs open or apps running?

Well, our brains work the same way.

When you have too many "open windows" or "apps running" your thought process slows down and your creativity diminishes. You feel overwhelmed and emotionally drained, even physically tired.

If you don't start closing some windows you will eventually crash like an overworked computer.

Many people are unaware of why they feel so drained, and why they crash and burn every so often. The answer is because they have too many windows open.

Here's a simple exercise that will transform your life. Meir Ezra taught this to me when I interviewed him on the show (Episode 76). If you do it, you will experience a sense of freedom that you may have never felt before. You will have more energy, focus, peace of mind, and, like many, you will feel reborn.

One reason why children are so full of life, filled with creativity and joy, is because they don't have so many tabs open.

Take out a piece of paper, and write down a list of ALL of the tabs you have currently open in your life. (You'll be surprised at how many you have!) Once you have your list, work your way down and start to either close each tab or set a date in your calendar to close it.

Work on closing one at a time. Don't go on to the next tab until you complete the one you started. The key is to focus on closing each one before moving on to the next one. Start training yourself to work on one *thing* before movinig onto the next.

Multitasking is a myth. It doesn't work effectively and leaves us feeling super drained and overwhelmed, and on top of that produces bad quality.

Go ahead, close some of those tabs in your life.

Don't let the notification pirates hijack your life

You are innocently writing an important article. You are highly focused. In the zone.

Then out of left field, you get a notification. It's like an itch that you need to scratch, so you quickly check it. One message, three YouTube videos and sixteen posts later, an hour has passed and you have lost focus on what you were doing. You have lost momentum. Momentum is one of the most powerful weapons in your productivity toolbox.

Email and social media messages are time-sucking parasites that feed off of you all day long. They leave you feeling drained and unproductive.

Don't let the notification pirates hijack your life.

Focus On One Thing

One thing I have always struggled with is focusing on one thing.

As an entrepreneur, we are naturally creative and driven to achieve greater things. Our greatest asset, however, can sometimes be our greatest enemy. If we don't channel our drive and energy and focus it on one project at a time, we can end up all over the place achieving nothing.

Think of an artist.

The artist has a blank canvas, and the possibilities are endless.

So many colors, shapes, sizes, space, and ideas but the artist needs to focus on a direction. The artist can't just throw all of the colors all over the place. (Although nowadays they would probably get away with calling it some funky name and selling it for millions!)

It's the same thing in business.

We must stay focused on a specific direction or we end up overwhelmed and emotionally drained.

When I started my telephone answering and virtual office company seven years ago, I started off super excited by the idea of building the biggest answering service and virtual office company in the UK. Then, after a couple of months, an opportunity presented itself that distracted me by its newness and freshness.

New opportunities excite me; they are like nice shiny objects tempting me; distracting me.

After a few months of "playing" with the new shiny object, I realized that I had neglected my core business and the new shiny object wasn't new and shiny anymore. So I re-focused on my core business. Until a few more months passed and another shiny object presented itself to me!

This became a pattern and I had to learn to ignore the shiny objects until I was able to experiment while keeping my finger on the pulse of my core business.

With my latest venture, Gefen Media Group, I get asked to resell other services all the time. It's tempting because it means we can create multiple revenue streams and offer even more value to our clients at the same time. The issue is that if we take our focus off our core service (getting people featured on and launching podcast shows) our quality and effectiveness will diminish. We will become 'everything to everyone' and ultimately a commodity that gets lost in the huge mesh of other unfocused businesses struggling to make it.

Shiny objects will present themselves to you along your journey as an entrepreneur. The more time you spend building your business the more frequently these shiny objects emerge. The trick is to notice them and not jump on them like a dog running after a stray cat in the street.

I'm not saying that you can't focus on a number of projects at a time.

Right now, I am running three separate businesses, producing a podcast show and writing a book. The key is to make sure that you have your finger on the pulse of each business. Don't sabotage your existing business for the shiny objects.

Most successful entrepreneurs credit their success to *staying focused and mastering one thing.*

I noticed that the best guests I had on my show were the ones that had *one clear message* they wanted to share. The ones that spoke about several different topics and dozens of ideas left my listeners overwhelmed and unsure of what to 'take home'.

When you have one core message you become memorable. You leave an impression. *You become remarkable.*

Stay Laser Focused

Joseph Isaacs has built and sold dozens of successful businesses.

Joseph has been successful in a dozen different industries. His various ventures have included a construction company, women's swimwear, a consulting firm, a telecommunications company, a property portfolio, a gourmet cheesecake manufacturer and even a bank. Yes, a bank.

When I asked him what the number one contributing factor to his success was he said *"Staying laser focused."*

He was able to be fully involved in one business, scale it, sell it and move on to the next business.

His latest exciting business venture, which he co-founded with his son is an interesting twist where popsicles meet alcoholic cocktails. Buzz Pop Cocktails is the first and only adult frozen drink in a push pop.

(He paid me to mention it in my book. Just kidding.)

Get Structured or Get Lost

Without a structured day, I get easily lost. I find myself checking emails, facebook feed, phone etc.

Self-help Addicts like me tend to do really badly without structure. My wife always wants to go on vacations, but for me, vacations used to be a nightmare. After a couple of days with no structure, I would get very restless and feel like I needed to *do something*. Doing nothing is okay when I plan on doing nothing. The problem is when I am not on vacation and I should be doing something. Being productive on vacation could be doing nothing at all. In fact it's crucial for someone who is usually extremely productive. It's great for re-energizing, refocusing, relaxing and spending quality time with the family. Vacation time for someone who is usually not very productive is a killer.

Look at children. They crave structure. Structure equals stability and security. As adults we are no different. We thrive within some sort of structured environment.

I hated school. School was a structured environment that I despised and didn't conform to. I'm not talking about fitting in to a structure built by others to mold you into what suits them or the general populace. I'm talking about creating *your own* structure.

What's interesting is that the reason Self-help Addicts tend to be extremely unstructured is because we hated having to 'fit in' with the structure society created for us. We felt imprisoned and confined against our will. We felt hampered, limited, restricted from being able to express who we really are.

They wanted us to be disciplined and follow the rules. We wanted to be free to choose our own version. That's the reason I believe that all these years I struggled to maintain a structured schedule. It's the reason I have been chasing the shiny objects and neglected certain responsibilities. It's the reason I have been inconsistent and unpredictable.

Ironically, it has been the lack of structure, discipline, consistency and commitment that has held me back from achieving my ultimate potential.

Until I finally came to the realisation that *freedom without limitations isn't freedom.*

I was floating through life.

Take for example a chess game where you decide that you don't like playing according to the rules so your pawn becomes a queen. You can do that but then you are no longer playing chess. In fact, the reason chess, (or any game) is enjoyable is because of the rules and restrictions. Without rules there is no challenge and without challenge there is no enjoyment.

Work in Focused Chunks of Time

I find that I am much more productive when I work in blocks of time. So for example while writing this book I blocked out 2 hours everyday where I became dead to the world and the world became dead to me (sorry for sounding so morbid). During that 2 hour block I switched everything off. All tabs on my laptop closed, phone on silent, notifications off. In fact I also found that blocking out the sound around me by wearing headphones and playing some light instrumental music really helped me focus!

Get highly focused by blocking out chunks of time and distractions.

If there is something you have been meaning to get done then block out a window of time and let everyone know that you are unavailable for the next x amount of time. Then switch off everything and just focus on getting it done. You will feel incredible.

We live in a noisy world filled with constant distractions. Messages, calls, ads, feeds, sounds, people, thoughts etc.

It's amazing when we can focus on one thing for a long period of time. Something magical happens. You lose sense of time and space ... even your sense of self (trippy I know). You get into this kind of transcendental meditative trance without trying to. I have periods where I completely lose any sense of anything. This is what's commonly known as the zone or *flow*. In fact, i'm experiencing it right now as I type this!

It's the secret sauce that bridges the gap between mediocrity and excellence. It takes you from the world of ordinary to the land of extraordinary. I believe it is the tool that unlocks the power of genius that we all have within us.

You can access this power anytime you want.

All you have to do is stay focused on the one thing you are trying to accomplish and lock yourself out from the world.

Or as I like to say *commit distraction suicide.*

Action Step: *Start closing down tabs that are still running in your life. Practice focusing on just one thing and shut everything else out.*

Man/Woman the Heck Up!

Growing old is mandatory; growing up is optional.

– Chili Davis

● ● ● ●

WARNING: This chapter may offend some of you.

I'm man enough to admit that I have spent most of my life living as a little boy. One day I decided to man the heck up.

It changed my life.

Now, what I'm about to say may come across as "too harsh." If it does, then feel free to skip this section. Come back to it when you're ready. It's a harsh truth. For those of you that are ready to hear it, it will change your life.

Okay, so here goes …

The generation we live in is filled with little children that look like grown adults.

People crying over the state of the economy, crying over who got elected, crying over spilled milk.

Taking selfies and posting it on social media to see how many people care enough about you to give you a "like."

You need to man the heck up.

You've got to stop being a little boy (or girl). At some point in your life, you've got to look yourself in the mirror and ask yourself:

"Am I a man or a boy?"

"Am I acting like a man or a little boy?"

"Are my actions like that of a woman or a little girl?"

"Am I talking like a man or a little boy?"

Excuses are for little boys and little girls. Real Men and Real Women don't make excuses. They get things done.

Real Men and Real Women are not afraid to voice their opinion. They say what they say because they believe in what they say. They're not afraid of what everyone else is going to think of them. They are not afraid of what everyone else might say about them.

Real Men and Real Women speak their mind and act based on what they believe in and not what they think other people will agree with or like.

Little boys and girls want attention. Real Men and Women don't need superficial attention. They get attention because people look up to them. Because people respect them. Not because they chase it or sell themselves for it.

Little boys and girls need permission to do things. They need validation. Real men and women don't need to be validated. They validate themselves. They don't need permission. They give themselves permission.

You gotta ask yourself a question. Are you tired of being a little boy or little girl?

Are you tired of having to please everyone around you?

Are you tired of feeling inferior?

Are you tired of being treated like a little girl?

Are you tired of wasting your energy trying to be someone you're not?

Then you need to start manning up. Start acting like a man. Stop whining. Stop expecting others to help you. Stop waiting for everyone to give you permission to be you. Stop trying to please everyone. Stop trying to get people to accept you.

When you wake up tomorrow morning you can make a decision.

Am I going to be a weak little boy today or am I going to be a powerful man?

Am I going to be a weak little girl or a powerful woman?

The choice is yours.

Action Step: *Next time you feel like you are thinking, speaking or acting like a little boy/girl stop yourself and ask how would a real man/woman think/speak/act.*

Pain Is Your Friend

I once woke up at 4 am to find myself paralyzed from the neck down.

It started with a slight discomfort in my lower back, and then I started feeling pain when I moved in a certain way.

The pain got worse when I got into bed and I found it hard to find a comfortable position to lie in.

Eventually, I fell asleep ...

... at 4 am I woke up in excruciating pain. I felt paralyzed from my neck down. I could not move my body without feeling a tremendous amount of pain.

My wife called an ambulance and I was taken to an emergency room where I was given an injection and some powerful pills.

Thank G-d I haven't experienced it since, but I want to share something that was going through my mind while all this was happening.

When I was lying there, unable to move, I realized how little I paid attention to the incredible gift of being able to move painlessly. I rarely give it a thought. My body works perfectly 99% of the time. My eyes, ears, lungs, teeth, kidneys, fingers, heart, feet, liver, neck, back, knees and so much more work like clockwork 24 hours a day, 7 days a week. And I go about my day as if that feat is worth nothing.

Pain has a way of getting us to recognize the gifts in our life. It brings about the greatest amount of clarity.

Why is it that when we experience pain we become so filled with gratitude, humility, and sensitivity?

Why is it that pain brings people together?

Why is it that pain motivates us more than anything else in the world?

I think the answer is because our ego blinds us.

Our ego prevents us from feeling grateful.
Our ego prevents us from having incredible relationships.
Our ego is our biggest enemy.

When we are in pain, our ego is silenced.

We feel helpless.
Our ego can't help us.

Pain gives us the ability to experience reality in it's fullest.
Pain is a friend we would rather avoid but sometimes, when the ego gets too big, we need a wake up call.
Pain is a beautiful part of life.

When we accept it, embrace it and learn from it we can experience life transformational growth.

From the Pits of Hell to the Peaks of Heaven

Tofe Evans was severely depressed. To the point of being suicidal. He would numb his pain with drugs.

He realized that when he ran, he felt relief. So he started running more often. Then he decided to run a marathon for charity. He became ever more driven. He channeled his pain and became an endurance athlete raising money for various charities

Today, he's one of only 100 people in the world to have run a 60km ultramarathon on Mt Everest.

He's endured a 24-hour run totaling 162km.

He's walked 100km while carrying 25L of water on his shoulders.

He ran 132km, lasting 24 hours on a treadmill.

He completed a 12-hour swim.

These are just some of the 40 endurance events he has completed in a mere year.

Tofe went from being extremely depressed with no direction in life to being nominated for the 2017 Young Australian of the Year Award.

When you channel your pain, you can harness a power that is unimaginable.

Turning Darkness into Light

When Kelsey Ramsden told me that she was grateful for having had Cancer, I nearly fell off my chair. (episode 84)

Kelsey was diagnosed with a rare case of cancer. But that didn't stop her from being named Canada's top female entrepreneur two years in a row and one of Canada's 100 most powerful women.

Kelsey is nothing short of a powerhouse.

She juggled raising three kids and grueling cancer treatments while building a 50 million dollar empire.

Kelsey said that having Cancer made her stronger and gave her the 'awakening' she needed.

Appreciate the struggle

There was once a boy who saw a butterfly struggling in a cocoon.

He felt sad that the butterfly was trapped and couldn't escape so he found a stick on the ground and started poking the cocoon. He finally managed to make a hole large enough for the "trapped" butterfly to escape.

To the boy's delight, the butterfly finally flew out.

The boy watched the butterfly flying freely and felt proud of his "heroism."

Suddenly, the butterfly started to spiral downward. It hit the ground. Its wings flapped a few more times desperately trying to take flight but to no avail. Then it lay still with no fight left in it.

The boy watched in horror.

He ran home crying.

His grandfather embraced him and asked what happened.

The boy explained the traumatic event.

His grandfather wiped his tears, looked him in the eyes and explained "My dear boy, the butterfly needed to struggle in the cocoon in order for its' wings to develop and build the strength to fly."

Sometimes, we need to let people struggle. It is the only way they will learn to grow and develop the skills to become the best version of themselves.

There is nothing wrong with struggling.

Pain Is Your Friend

Everything in creation experiences resistance in order to grow.

Muscle growth comes from endurance. Lifting a weight that doesn't create resistance won't produce bigger muscles.

Working through struggles in a relationship makes the relationship stronger.

Pushing yourself past your comfort zone is the only way to achieve real growth.

Temporary pain can often bring the best out of us.

Action Step: *The next time you feel pain. Thank it.*

Get Comfortable With Being Uncomfortable

Life begins at the end of your comfort zone.

– Neale Donald Walsch

● ● ● ● ●

Without a doubt, my most successful accomplishments have come from doing things that were uncomfortable.

Celebrating 10 years with my wonderful wife didn't come from being comfortable all the time. Great marriages are hard work. It required stepping out of my comfort zone many times, on a daily basis.

Sharing my space. Giving in to someone else's wishes. Caring about someone other than myself.

Waiting for her. Listening to her. Giving to her. Being with her. Caring for her.

Not being able to do whatever I want to do whenever I want with whomever I want.

It's a life of sacrifice. It's a committed life.

The reward, however, is immense.

True love does not come without hardships. True love is earned. But there is nothing in this universe that compares to true love.

I never fell in love.

I climbed a large mountain to reach the level of love I have for my wife.

And I'm still climbing.

You can fall into fantasy. You can't fall in love.

Being a father to four children is by far the most rewarding challenge I have confronted in my life.

Having children is not something I would do if I lived only in my comfort zone.

Raising children to be leaders (in their own right) is not something I would be able to do in my comfort zone.

Building a relationship with each of my children is not something I would be able to do in my comfort zone.

If you have children, you know exactly what I mean.

Bedtime. Bath time. School time. Get Dressed time. Dinner time. Brush teeth time. Listen to your mother time. Clean up your room time. No, you can't have that time. Don't answer back time. Teenage time. Growing up time. Leaving home time.

Children are the cause of the most amount of stress you will ever have in your life.

But they are also the cause of the most amount of eternal pleasure you can ever hope for.

Launching and growing multiple businesses. Hosting a podcast show. Speaking at events. Writing a book. These are some of my major accomplishments that I wouldn't have even considered, had I stayed in my comfort zone.

Self-help-addicts spend most of their time within their comfort zone.

Creators spend most of their time expanding their comfort zone.

Your comfort zone is the barrier to entry to all the things you wish to accomplish in life, but are afraid to do.

Self-help addicts live in a small space and are held captive there by fear, doubt, and laziness.

Every time you break down the wall of your comfort zone, it expands. The more your comfort zone expands the bigger space you have to play in.

The first time you break the wall requires a lot of effort, courage, and bravery. But with each successive time, breaking down the wall becomes easier.

Eventually, you get to the point where your comfort zone is so big that you can't see the walls anymore.

Life goes from being restrictive to expansive.

Scarcity becomes abundance. Fears become opportunities. The world becomes your playground.

A formula for connecting with anyone

I had the pleasure of interviewing a guy by the name of Anil Gupta (episode 60) who shared his incredible story of how he went from being suicidal to teaching happiness on Richard Branson's Necker Island!

Anil casually mentioned that he beat Richard Branson in a game of tennis. He talked about how he gave parenting advice to Mike Tyson (without getting his ear chewed off!) He also got to spend time with Tony Robbins on his private jet.

How does Anil manage to get so close with all these powerful performers? He said it had to do with 3 things:

Be Fearless. Don't be afraid to approach people you admire and strike up a conversation.

Be Playful. Don't take yourself so seriously. Celebrities like people who are genuine and are fun to be around. Treat them like you would a good friend. Don't make them into some sort of idol.

Learn to Listen. The best conversationalists are the ones that know how to listen intensely. Become genuinely interested in other people and listen to what excites them.

The Elevator Experiment

Anil also shared a very powerful way to practice being fearless.

I call it *"The Elevator Experiment."*

We all know how awkward it is when you step into an elevator with strangers. Everyone avoids eye contact and "disappears" into the "safety" of their smartphones (or they just stare at their feet).

Anil walks into an elevator full of people and announces "Hey guys, sorry I'm late to this meeting!"

People laugh. The awkwardness fades. A conversation is started. Humans interact.

New connections are made. Relationships are built.

So... the next time you step into an elevator ...try it.

What's the worst that can happen?

Action Step: Do something extremely uncomfortable every day for 30 days

Abundance vs. Scarcity Mindset

Abundance is not something we acquire. It is something we tune into.

– Wayne Dyer

• • • • •

Growing up, I remember my father complaining that things were "too expensive." He was always scared of how his business was doing. It drove him to panic attacks, and it had a major carry-over effect on me.

I remember many arguments between my mother and father over money. Although I grew up in a middle-class home, it seemed as if we never had "enough" and my father was constantly worried sick about his financial situation.

He reacted by running away and hiding from it. He owned a few grocery stores but very rarely spent time in them. He was too scared to find out how much money he really had.

It instilled me with the false belief that money is limited and created within me high levels of anxiety over money.

It took me many years to challenge this false belief and switch from a scarcity mindset to a mindset of abundance.

I'm the oldest in my family, and we have videos of me hitting my younger brother off his bike with a broom.

I had a major scarcity mindset from a very young age.

Interestingly, my oldest son Elisha developed a scarcity mindset too when his younger brother Gabriel was born. Gabriel, on the other hand, seemed to have an abundance mindset. He always wanted his older brother to have the things that he had. For example, every time I would buy something for Gabriel he would say "What about Elisha?"

I think it has to do with the fact that Elisha was used to being the only child for the first year of his life and wasn't used to sharing his parents, toys, space etc. with someone else. Gabriel, on the other hand, came into the world with someone already there. To him, nothing was "taken away."

As children, we are born into a world that is gigantinormous (in the words of my three-year old) and everything is new and exciting. There is so much of everything. We delight in each new thing we experience. But then one day, we encounter another child who wants to play with one of our toys.

We cry.

Our parents say, "You must share."

We cry some more.

We don't know if we will ever get it back. We don't know if the other child will break it. We are scared we will lose it and never have it again. We don't know that you can just go and buy it again at the local toy store.

Hopefully, we grow up and come to realise that there is enough for everyone in this world. Some people adopt the abundance mindset early on. For others, it takes many years.

And for many , they die with a scarcity mindset.

From broke to $500,000 in just two years

When I interviewed Jenn Scalia on my show (episode 28), she shared her story of how she went from being completely broke, divorced and raising a son in her parents home to amassing half a million dollars in just two years!

When I asked her what changed, she responded with just one word.

Mindset.

She worked so hard on changing her mindset that she blocked her own uncle on Facebook because he was so negative.

Jenn even claims that getting divorced was the best business decision she ever made.

She feels that having the right mindset is more important than having the right skills.

Don't Panic - there's enough for everyone!

We live in a world of abundance.

It may seem that there is a lack of food, money, and resources but actually, there is enough for everyone to have enough. Too often, people have a scarcity mindset, which leads to competitiveness, fear, and greed.

The world is only as limited as you make it out to be, and, on the flip-side, it's as abundant as you believe it is.

People with a scarcity mindset are always worried about competition. As a result, they talk themselves out of making more money. They complain about things like the government or the state of the economy. They are very mistaken. The world is open to reap the abundant resources that are available for anyone who is open to receive it at any time.

During times of recession, people have become very wealthy.

The sad fact is that if the world changed its mindset and realized how much abundance there was, nobody would starve. Nobody would be homeless.

As a civilization, we have underestimated ourselves.

There are currently 7.5 billion people in this world. Imagine what we could do if we all worked with one another instead of against one another!

Imagine if all countries shared their resources and worked together in an alliance to make the world, as a whole, a better place for everyone!

The scarcity mindset creates fear, and fear leads to wars. Countries feel threatened by other countries and end up spending an insane amount of money just protecting themselves. The US spent over $600 billion in 2015 on their military and defense budget! Can you imagine how that kind of money could be spent in a world that embraces the abundance mindset?!

There would be no more hunger in this world!

This all comes down to a scarcity mindset. If the whole world joined together in one big partnership, we would all be wealthy and there would be an abundance for everyone.

Although we can't change the way the whole world thinks, *we can change our own mindset.*

So from this moment on, don't focus on what's lacking in the world, but rather what is available. Adopt an abundance mindset and you will start to see an abundance come your way.

Be prepared to have more than you could ever imagine!

Action Step: *Start looking at everything as an opportunity. Recognize how much there is rather than what's lacking.*

Rewrite Your Script

"You are the author of your life, so make it a bestseller."

– Daniel Gefen

• • • • •

As self-help addicts we tend to have poorly written scripts. Some of them we wrote ourselves, and some we adopted from others, like our parents or teachers.

For me, one of the scripts I wrote for myself when I was young was "I'm not an early riser."

I wrote that script in my younger years and that was the script that I followed.

Every day, I would wake up and the alarm would go off, and like clockwork, I switched it off, rolled over, and went back to sleep.

After all, *I'm not an early riser.*

I lived by that script.

One day, after being particularly fed up with this endlessly repeating cycle, I had a flash of insight: *What if I just...change the script?*

I simply decided from then on I would consider myself an early riser. And to prove it, I was going to do it.

So that night, I set my alarm for 6:15 am and the following morning, almost automatically, I switched off the alarm and got out of bed.

There were still the same thoughts going on in my head.

"I'm so tired."

"I won't be productive today."

"It's too dark and cold outside."

"I just need another 20 minutes."

But there was one thought that answered all of them — "I'm an early riser!"

I followed the script that I wrote.

It worked so well that I started changing any script I didn't like.

"I'm scared of public speaking" to "I'm a great public speaker."
"I'm a lazy person" to "I'm a highly productive person."
"I'm impatient" to "I'm a patient person."

I started living by the NEW scripts that I wrote for myself!

The cool thing is that we can trick our brain into thinking we are something else, and, as if by magic, *we start becoming that very person.*

Don't like your personality? You can literally *choose your own personality.*
Don't like feeling a certain way? *Become someone who doesn't feel that way.*
Don't like your current behaviors or habits? *Choose different ones.*

So the question you should ask yourself is "What script have I written for myself?"

What have you repeated to yourself over the years that has boxed you in and confined you to define who you are?

Remember: *You can change your script whenever you want.*

Consistency is Key

Writing the script is the first step. It's like writing down some goals only to look back at them after a few months and wonder why you never accomplished them.

It's frustrating.

We tell ourselves that goal-setting doesn't work.

We decide that it's a waste of time.

New Year's resolutions are a perfect example. Everyone sets goals at the beginning of the year. They write new scripts. But after a few weeks or months, they fall back to following their old scripts.

The reason why New Year's resolutions rarely work is because writing your new script is only the first part of the equation to transform your life and it happens to be the easy part. All you have to do is take out a piece of paper and write down some goals.

Very little effort is involved.

The hard part is taking the action. And it isn't just taking action singularly, but rather taking consistent action.

The key word here is *consistent*.

The excitement gives you a boost. The newness and freshness make it easier to take that first action

Getting up early on the 2nd of January is much easier than getting up early on the 31st of December.

Going to the gym the first couple of times may be easier because the excitement and newness get you going. The hard part is keeping it up after the first couple of times.

Do you keep going to the gym even though you don't really feel like going?

Do you keep waking up early and get out of your bed even though you feel like staying in your warm bed?

Do you keep holding your tongue when you feel like shouting at your spouse?

Real transformation in your life requires hard work. It doesn't come easy. As Self-help Addicts one of the symptoms is that we expect things to come easy. We expect there to be a secret key or some quick fix solution. But the simple fact is that real transformation comes through taking consistent action.

The brain is very powerful. Our brain has been programmed with old scripts. It will say things like:

"You are not an early riser, so you should stay in bed."
"You are not a patient person, you should be getting frustrated now."
"You are not a calm person, you should be getting angry right now."
"You're not a consistent person, you should give up."

Your brain has been programmed that way.

One of the scripts I wrote was "I am an inconsistent person, so when I make goals I don't keep them."

I changed that script by writing a new one. "I am a consistent person, so when I make goals I keep them."

Then I wrote down some goals that I knew I could keep and I reinforced my new script with action. Consistent action.

The only way to change the voices in your head is by taking action that goes against what the voices are saying. Eventually, if you take enough action, something magical happens — your mind shifts and the voices in your head start to shift too.

Escape From The Matrix

"The Matrix was not a movie, it was a documentary."

Tom Bilyeu was my dream guest. I had been watching his show "Impact Theory" for years and fell in love with his obsessive quest for mastering the mind.

Tom's ability to *rewrite the script* allowed him to build the second fastest growing US company in 2014. Quest Nutrition grew by 57,000% in year three and was valued at over a billion dollars within just five years!

He has embarked on a journey to follow the white rabbit, take the red pill, escape from the Matrix and help others do the same.

"To me, the brain IS the Matrix. And just like once you wake up in the Matrix you can bend it to your will, the brain will bend to your will and allow you to do things you never thought possible.

But first, you have to believe."

Action Step: *Start re-writing some of your negative scripts. Take out a piece of paper and jot down some that keep creeping up and re-write them.*

Ups And Downs

*"What the caterpillar calls the end,
the rest of the world calls a butterfly."*

– Lao Tsu

• • • • •

I was having one of my "down days" when, unsurprisingly, my guest canceled on me three minutes before we were supposed to go live (when it rains, it pours.)

He wasn't feeling up to it (and nor was I).

I think he had a pretty rough night, and so he sent me a message letting me know that he felt exhausted.

He gave me two options.

Either we could do the interview, but it would probably not be great quality, or we can reschedule for another time. I was frustrated because I had already spent two hours doing my research on him and putting together the intro.

I was having a really crappy day. It was just was one of those days where I didn't get much done. I just felt so low and for no particular reason.

I decided to reschedule the episode.

But instead of going home and binging on YouTube videos I decided to do a solo episode and share how I felt. I received so much feedback about that 15-minute solo episode from people who really resonated with what I said.

Here's what I shared in that episode:

" ... you know how you always see me full of energy? I'm usually buzzing away, right?

You watch my Facebook lives. You've seen my posts and my pictures on social media and I portray this very energetic full of life positive productive guy. Well, here's the thing...

There' are two sides to every story. There are two sides to every picture. What you don't see, is the Daniel Gefen you know getting up and feeling like crap and then pulling the covers over my head thinking "I don't want to get up today." You don't see that part of me. You don't see the part of me not being able to handle a situation and just blowing up and going crazy for no reason.

The truth is that people just want other people to like them.

You don't want people to see the bad side of you. You want people to see the good side and that's why I have a love-hate relationship with social media because I feel like it's so easy to be fake. It's just so easy to put on a show for everybody else.

The problem is that everybody thinks that everybody else has it better than they do. They look at their Instagram and their Facebook and they think "oOh, wow look at them. Look at the vacation they went on," and "Wow, look at their perfect family. They look so happy." And "It looks like their business is thriving."

The truth is, it's nonsense. It's baloney.
Because you don't see the full picture.
You just see a *small slice.*
You see that *snapshot.*

You see a snapshot of the perfect couple on the beach. But what you don't see is what happened before they got to the beach. She was running late and he's shouting.
"Come on. What are you doing why are you taking so long!"
She's yelling back "What do you mean I need to get my stuff?"
"But you took 20 minutes already, and I want to get to the beach before the sun sets!"

Back and forth.

And you don't see the kids beating each other up in the background ...
"What are you doing. Leave him alone! You're punished!"
You don't see all of that.
That's the *real stuff. That's life.*

If you asked me "Daniel, do you have a happy marriage"?

My answer would be "Yes, I have a happy marriage, and I love my wife and I love my children and I would do anything for them."

But I would be lying if I told you that it was all singing birds and rose petals all day. It's not. It's life. *Get real.*"

But we don't post that stuff.
We don't post an argument we have with our spouse.
We don't post an episode of us losing control with our kids.
We don't post a picture of ourselves looking like crap.

We don't post those things because, let's face it, *we want to show everybody how "perfect"' our lives are.*

I struggled my whole life. I still do. I work on myself daily. When I started my podcast show I recorded the first episode 17 times because I couldn't get one sentence out. As I'm talking into the mic right now, I'm shocked that I'm able to speak for nine minutes straight and I haven't pressed stop. I haven't pressed the pause button because maybe I shouldn't have said that. Or maybe let me just edit that part out...

No, I'm speaking from my heart. And that didn't come just because I got in front of a mike and suddenly I was able to speak naturally. It didn't happen like that.

I recorded that first episode 17 times because I couldn't speak for 30 seconds without stopping the recording because I felt like it just wasn't good enough or because I messed up or I said something that I shouldn't have said.

And I guarantee you that every single person that you look up to, every person you admire, they are the same way. They get into fights. They have down days. They do things they regret.

But I guess it's the nature of people who are in the public eye to show only the positive, the great stuff. You don't get to see the struggle. People watch Gary Vaynerchuk, for example. They see his YouTube videos and they see everything he does. Wow. How does he do that?

You don't see what goes on behind closed doors. You also didn't see the Gary Vaynerchuk before he became Gary Vaynerchuk. You didn't see when he first started producing videos. He sucked. He was really really bad at producing videos but now he's great.

When you watch someone get up and rock the stage, I guarantee you that the first time they got on stage they didn't. I guarantee you they failed multiple times because that's the nature of the beast. If you really want to get good at something then you've got to fail a bunch of times.

Before Alice got to Wonderland she had to fall.

There's nothing wrong with having a down day.

Some people say you've got to push yourself. You know what? I don't agree with that.

I don't think you have to push yourself all the time. I think everybody's different and I think you have to know yourself really, really well. Nobody can tell you what to do. Nobody can say "Oh, you should do this" or "You should do that."

No, you should do what *you* feel is right. That's what I've learned to do. I've learned that I have to trust myself. I have to really dig deep and ask myself "Daniel, are you BSing yourself or are you being real right now."

And *as long as I'm being real, I don't care what anybody thinks.*

As long as you are being real with who you really are then it doesn't matter what anybody else tells you or what they think of you. If you feel like you genuinely need to take the day off and take a walk, go for a run, or visit the beach if that's what you need to do right now to unwind and relax and just take time off — then do it!

Trust your instinct; trust your gut.

Nobody knows you better than yourself.

Because here's what's going to happen if you don't, and I'm speaking from my own experience, when you push yourself too much, when you listen to everybody else and you push yourself even though you feel that you just can't do it, when your body is telling you you're tired, take time off and you ignore it and push yourself all you are doing is you're making it worse because what's going to happen is eventually *you're going to snap.*

You snap.

People have nervous breakdowns for that reason. People snap because they kept pushing themselves when they shouldn't have pushed themselves. They should have taken that nap during the day, overslept, or just taken the day off. Because if your body is telling you something, if your inner voice is saying something to you then listen to it. *It's always right.*

There are different voices and I've started to learn to differentiate between the voices in my head.

There are sometimes voices in my head that say "Oh, Daniel, you shouldn't do that" or "You're never going to be able to do that" or "You're going to fail."

I know those voices. I recognize them. They've been in my head my whole life, and I know that those are the voices I need to ignore. I tell them to shut up. I'm going to do it anyway.

But then there's that inner, quieter voice. It may sound weird, but usually, the voices that are lying to you, the voices that are not coming from your inner-self are usually very loud. They're usually screaming at you. They usually sound agitated.

But when it comes from your inner voice it's usually very quiet, soft-spoken, and patient. When you recognize that voice, that's the voice to listen to. Because whenever I've ignored that voice it's always backfired on me. And whenever I listen to that voice, it's worked out. You may not see the results immediately, but long term you will. You'll see that if you listen to that voice, and ignore the loud voices, the quiet voice will change your life.

When I say that "I had a down day today," it doesn't mean that I regret my day. I don't regret my day and I don't think that I'm bad because I didn't "do much" today. I'm completely fine. I had a down day, today. I accept myself for who I am, and I accept the fact that I'm allowed to have days off. It's perfectly normal and reasonable. There's nothing wrong with it.

The fact that my guest canceled on me today happened because I needed to share this. I'm grateful that my guest canceled, so I can share this incredibly important message. One that I will probably listen back to when I'm having another down day."

Zombie Mode

When you get hyper-focused, you enter "The Zone," at the other end of the spectrum there is a place I sometimes find myself in which I call "Zombie Mode."

Zombie Mode is when you are in this trance-like, heavily depressed, lazy state. You just feel heavy. All motivation gets sucked out of you. You feel almost lifeless. I hate when I get into this state, and while I'm in it, I feel like there is no way out of it. Sometimes I feel like there's just no point to life anymore when I'm in this state.

I have always wondered how I ever got into Zombie Mode in the first place.

Here's my five top causes for Zombie Mode:

1. **Oversleeping**

   I find that if I get more than eight hours of sleep my body feels stiff, my mind feels groggy, and I find myself in Zombie Mode. Sometimes if I take a nap in the middle of the day I find myself in Zombie Mode too. Sleeping on an airplane almost always gets me into Zombie Mode!

2. **Overeating**

   Usually, after I eat a high carb meal (or I just stuff my face) my body feels physically heavier, and I end up in Zombie Mode.

3. **Overthinking**

   I call this "Stinking Thinking." When my brain goes into overdrive and I get overwhelmed by my thinking, my mind short circuits. I usually end up finding myself in Zombie Mode.

4. **Overheating**

   If I have been inside for too long without any open windows my body overheats, slows down and I tend to get into Zombie Mode.

5. **Overscreening**

   Okay, "Overscreening" is definitely a made-up word but I couldn't find a better word for it (lemme know if you come up with a better one.) This is when I have been staring at a screen for too long. It could be working on my laptop or scrolling through my social feed on my cell phone. After a certain period of time, my eyes start to glaze over and I enter into the dreaded Zombie Mode.

The Cure For Zombie Mode

Interestingly enough, the cure is actually very simple. It's simple, but it feels impossible when you're in Zombie Mode. In fact, it's the last thing you want to do.

The Zombie wants to curl up and give up on life. The Zombie wants to stay in a dark warm lonely place. The Zombie will try to convince you that you simply cannot do anything.

DON'T LISTEN TO THE ZOMBIE!

The cure for me usually consists of three main ingredients:
1. Fresh Air
2. Movement
3. Drinking Water

To avoid getting into Zombie Mode ...
- Sleep right
- Eat healthy
- Avoid overthinking
- Step away from your device (put away your phone)
- Get outside
- Go for a walk
- Drink plenty of water

Your Zombie will hate me for this. You will love me for it.

Action Step: *The next time you are feeling low, accept it and recognize it's a temporary situation. Do something you enjoy and just be okay with where you are at that moment.*

Keeping Things In Perspective

We can complain because rose bushes have thorns, or rejoice because thorns have roses.

– Alphonse Karr

● ● ● ● ●

One of the scariest moments of my life was when I thought I was going to lose my wife.

It was about 3 p.m. I was in my office busy with work, and I get a phone call. It's my wife.

She says she can't breathe.

I said, "What? What do you mean?"

She whispers "I can't breathe."

She's barely talking and I just keep asking "What do you mean you can't breathe? Why can't your breathe?!"

She responds, barely able to get the words out her mouth, "The ambulance is on its way"

Then hangs up the phone.

I freaked out.

I ran out of my office. Stopped everything. Jumped into my car and raced home. There are thoughts in my head like, "Am I about to lose the most precious person in my life?" and "Is that really going to happen right now?"

I couldn't stop thinking the worst. What's going to happen with the kids? I don't want to be alone. I love her too much. I can't lose her like this. *What's going to happen?*

I get home and the ambulance is already there. My wife is being wheeled out, and they've got an oxygen mask on her face.

I start yelling, "What the hell happened?"

The neighbor comes up to me and explains, "Your wife inhaled chlorine."

We have a swimming pool and she was refilling the pool with chlorine from a container that was left out in the sun. When she opened the canister, it blew up in her face.

They're rushing her to the hospital, and I'm stuck at home. I don't know how to react. I'm not afforded the luxury to panic. I've got to be calm for the kids; I've got to put them to bed. In the meantime, my head is racing. What's happening to my wife? I need to be with my wife, but I need to be with my kids. It's the scariest thing.

I just felt completely *powerless*. You know what I mean? Just powerless. Finally, I put the kids to bed and I text my wife.

"Is everything okay?"

She responds, "Yeah, I'm basically hooked up to a machine, and they're taking X-rays of my lungs. They're going to keep me here overnight."

I ended up pacing through my bedroom and .... this is going to sound weird but ... I smelled her clothes. I smelled my wife's clothes and I literally felt like I was going to just break down because I felt I couldn't lose her. I can't lose her.

I somehow fell asleep and the next morning, I called her up. She picked up the phone and told me that they took her off the machine. Thank God. Thank God she's breathing again on her own. "It's not easy to breathe but it's okay," she says. Her lungs are thankfully clear, and they're just keeping her for a few more hours. Then I'll be able to come and pick her up.

I remember getting into the car to pick up my wife. As I'm driving, I started thinking to myself, "Why do I worry about such stupid things like parking tickets, getting cut off on the road, and slow Wi-Fi!"

Why does it take almost losing a loved one to get to that wakeup call where you realize that *most things are not that big of a deal.*

When we're not looking at the big picture, and we're stuck in the nitty-gritty of things, then the little things get blown out of proportion.

What's the goal? We're only here for a certain period of time and that's it.

When you die, what do you want to leave behind?

What do you want to be remembered by?

What legacy do you want to leave?

Do you want to be the person who just read lots of books, took in lots of information, tried lots of things and followed lots of people?

Or do you want to be the person that inspired others to change their lives?

I guarantee you, if every day you focus on the important things, the things that really mean the world to you, the ones that are truly worth living for and dying for, if you focus on those things, then all the other stuff won't matter anymore. It just won't. Any dream that you have, whether it's speaking on stage or asking someone out on a date, those fears that you have, they're silly. They are. They're just silly little thoughts.

"What happens if I forget my lines…"
"What happens if I make a fool out of myself?"
"What if she says no?"

Who cares?! So what?! What's the worst that will happen?

Are you going to die? No. You're not.

Instead of focusing on the little negative things that might happen focus instead on the *big things* that might happen.

"What if I inspire people to take major action in their lives?"
"What if I get on stage and I get a standing ovation?"
"What if she says yes?"

In that moment, while I was driving to pick up my wife, if you told me that I had just received a massive bill in the mail I wouldn't care. I just wanted my wife to come home. That's all I cared about. I was focused on the big picture.

Perspective is everything.

Gratitude Kills Depression

It's impossible to be grateful and depressed at the same time.

Try it.

When I am feeling low I think about all the wonderful things I have in my life.

I go on a mental journey picturing all the gifts I have in my life.

I think about how fortunate I truly am to be alive. I think about all the people suffering.

People dying of starvation. People homeless. People who have lost loved ones. People with poor health. People who suffer from mental illnesses.

I think about what it would be like to live without legs, unable to run. Without my eyesight, unable to see what my children look like. Without the ability to hear sounds of the waves. I picture my life with all the things I have, and I realise that life is good when put in the right perspective.

Everything is relative.

Sad was the man who lost his shoes until he saw the man who lost his legs

When I am grateful I am a better husband, boss, father, son, and friend. When you appreciate others you light up their souls. You become a rare gem in their life.

Most people think about themselves.

They expect others to do for them. They expect life to give them what they need. They have this feeling of entitlement. So when you show appreciation, you become a breath of fresh air. You become the life of their party.

But most importantly, when you appreciate *yourself*, you stop beating yourself up. When you start praising yourself and stop being so hard on yourself you learn to love yourself more.

Gratitude is the ultimate cure for depression. (Some people do require medication or formal therapy for depression. Obviously, I am not speaking about them.)

Getting High and Staying High

... without drugs :)

The key to getting high and staying high is becoming a giver instead of a taker.

Focus on how you can help others, instead of how others can help you.

Earning a million dollars is nowhere near as fulfilling as giving away a million dollars.

Giving is a powerful drug.

It's the most powerful drug in the world.

Giving a smile to someone who feels down is like giving someone who is drowning CPR.

You can literally revive someone, bring them back to life, just by giving them a warm smile. Be the first to greet others instead of waiting for others to greet you. Look for solutions to other people's problems and I guarantee you will become wealthy.

When you are having a down day (and we all have a down day from time to time), find someone you can help. Get out of your rut and call someone who needs cheering up. Go visit someone in hospital. Send someone a positive message. Buy someone a gift.

There's no quicker way to get out of a dark place than by creating a spark of light in someone else's life.

It's much easier to motivate others than to motivate yourself. So find somebody to motivate. Be prepared to feel like a changed person.

Go ignite others and set yourself on fire.

Action Step: *Get into a habit of writing down gratitude lists. Start seeing the bigger picture in every detail.*

Becoming a Superhero

You have a superhero in you, and only you know what your superpowers are.

– Daniel Gefen

● ● ● ● ●

We all have the ability to become superheroes in our own world.

No, I'm not going to tell you how to fly like Superman or climb skyscrapers like Spiderman.

That's not so impressive. Birds can fly and monkeys can climb trees.

As humans, we have something infinitely more powerful and important.

We have something called "free choice."

Every time we are given a choice to grow and become better people, we are exercising a superpower.

Each of us has different struggles. Some, struggle with healthy eating and exercising. Others struggle with not getting angry and saying nasty things to the people we love. Some of us struggle with trying to pay the bills each month. The list goes on.

One thing I struggle with is waking up early in the morning. For me, it's a battle every single day. My bed becomes my war zone. Sometimes I fail. My warm covers are just too tempting for me to leave. I roll over and fall back to sleep only to feel frustrated later with myself. Sometimes I succeed and break out of my comfort zone. I push myself mentally and physically to break free from my laziness. In those moments, I become a superhero.

When my wife gets upset and we, disagree, sometimes I'm tempted to put her down or blame her. Instead, I hold my tongue. I take a walk. I cool off. I put myself in her shoes. I remind myself how much I love her. I tell her how much I love her. In those moments, I am a superhero.

Sometimes when I have had a hectic day and my kids need my attention, I don't want to give to them. I feel like I need to escape. I become impatient and distant. But I stop myself and put my feelings on hold. I force myself to be present even though I don't want to be. I tuck them in their beds and read them a bedtime story. I kiss them goodnight and tell them I love them. In those moments, I am their superhero.

Red capes and magical powers don't make us superheroes.

Daily struggles, overcoming temptations, pushing boundaries, breaking out of our comfort zones, sacrificing short-term gains for long-term wins, standing for what we believe in, and not what we think others want us to be, giving and receiving selflessly, THAT'S what makes us superheroes!

It's within the mundane activities that we can truly shape our destiny. It's the small consistent choices we make that create the biggest impact in our lives.

You have a superhero in you and only you know what your superpowers are.

The 4-Minute Mile

Sir Roger Bannister was the first man to run a mile in under four minutes. Up until he did it in 1954, most people thought the four-minute mark was impossible to break. They thought the human body couldn't physically go that fast – that it would collapse under the pressure.

No-one could run a mile in less than four minutes.

It was impossible.

You were crazy to even try.

That was, until Bannister proved everyone wrong.

What's most interesting about this story is that once Bannister proved it could be done, something extraordinary happened.

All of a sudden, many people were breaking the record of running a mile in under four minutes - the same people who believed that it was impossible before Bannister proved them wrong!

This is so fascinating because it proves that we are only as limited as we choose to believe we are.

We have all heard stories of people who under extreme situations have managed to survive against all odds. People have managed to go without food and water for extreme periods of time. There have been many incidents that were "unexplainable" where even disabled people turned into superheroes. A blind man who saves a blind woman from a burning house. A man who weighed just 150 pounds carrying four soldiers off the battlefield. A girl lifting a car to save her father. And many other instances where mere mortals go beyond their seemingly physical limitations and do incredible superhuman feats.

Our limitations exist only in our mind.

Action Steps: *Practise pushing your limitations. Discover what your unique superpowers are.*

Be Memorable

"For me, being memorable is more important than winning."

– Ricki Lake

● ● ● ● ●

The Internet has introduced powerful tools to connect millions of people with the simple click of a button. An email, a tweet, a private message, a post. Within seconds, you can reach more people than your ancestors did in their lifetimes.

The world has become a "numbers game," but *nobody cares about being a number.*

The same tools you have at your disposal are easily accessible to the other seven billion people on this planet, which means that everyone is being bombarded with emails, tweets, messages and ads on a daily basis. The way people act online reminds me of how people act when driving their cars. Normal, well mannered people step into their cars and evolve into insensitive masters of metal. All of a sudden, everyone else becomes objects to avoid, ignore, honk at, shout out, cut off, and curse at. *The world has become faceless, but humans crave human interaction.*

I started to realize the power of human interaction and developing deep relationships when I began my podcast. It"s amazing what sixty minutes of talking to someone can actually do for a relationship. I make an effort to keep in touch with everyone I interview. They are all busy people, and are probably bombarded with messages from fans trying to connect.

But here's the secret: *They are human beings. And all human beings crave deep, meaningful relationships.*

How many times has someone tried to get your attention with the same lazy, cold piece of spam? If it doesn't work to get your attention then why try using it to get the attention of others? The Internet has made people lazy. It"s so easy to mass message or post quick meaningless things in the hope that a percentage of the masses will react.

Lazy people hope for the best. Successful people work hard to make things happen.

Here are some ways you can become memorable:

Be more intimate

Instead of posting "Happy Birthday" on someone's Facebook timeline and getting lost in the masses, take sixty seconds and send them a happy birthday video message. They will remember you for it! Reach out to people one-on-one and start a personal conversation. Dare I say it—pick up the phone and call people! Instead of commenting on other people's posts with the same old one word replies like "cool" or "#Truth," put some time into sharing how their post had an impact on you.

Dig deeper

Instead of posting useless, mindless one liners, post something deep and interactive. Get personal and vulnerable. Share parts of yourself you have never shared publicly (not everything.)

Become a Giftologist

Surprise people by sending them a gift in the mail.

Have you ever received a gift from someone totally at random that made your heart melt? How did it make you feel? What did you think of that person? Do you still remember them?

I had the pleasure of having John Ruhlin on my show (episode 109). John has a remarkable story and shared the key to building a network of die hard fans.

He went from being an Ohio farm boy to becoming the greatest seller in Cutco"s 68 year history out of 1.5 million other reps and distributors!

How? By mastering the art and science of giving gifts.

He's the bestselling author of the transformational book titled "Giftology," "The art and science of using gifts to cut through the noise, increase referrals and strengthen retention."

He shared with me a story that shifted my whole mindset and changed my perspective on the importance of gift giving.

John was meeting a guy by the name of Cameron Herold, called "the man executives turn to for business advice by CNN." (He's a good friend and mentor of mine). The plan was to take Cameron out for dinner and then to a basketball game.

John found out that Cameron loves clothes from Brooks Brothers so he went to the local branch and bought every single item they had in his size. EVERY SINGLE ITEM! The total cost was $7,000 and it took an hour to pack it all up into his SUV. He then set up all the clothes in the hotel room that Cameron was going to stay in. It looked like a Brooks Brothers store!

When Cameron landed, he was tired as his flight was delayed, and he texted John saying that he may not be up to meet. John told him to go to his room, take a shower, and let him know how he felt after.

John waited in the lobby of the Ritz. Cameron came down after a few minutes with his face glowing and eyes lit up. He couldn't believe what John had done. Cameron refused to accept it all, but said he was so touched that he would pay John for the clothes he wanted. They ended up talking for hours.

Anywhere Cameron goes he talks about John. He promotes John"s book and company to all of his clients and audiences he speaks to around the world.

Cameron has become a walking billboard for John.

In fact it was Cameron that introduced me to John and suggested that he come on my show :) Isn't it incredible what one thoughtful gift can do? The impact is unimaginable.

When I asked John how much that one gesture was worth monetarily, he said it must be in the high six figures so far!

"I couldn't have received that kind of response if I spent a million dollars on advertising!" He said.

I had another guest on my show that shared a similar experience. Yoav Adomi, co- founder of Swiftic (the world's leading do-it-yourself mobile app solution) told me he was trying to get hold of the CEO of a Fortune 500 corporation. Emails and phone calls went unreturned. So he did some research and found out that her greatest obsession was her dog. She loved her dog more than anything else in the world. She would constantly post pictures of her dog on social, and even created a room for him in corporate headquarters so he wasn't left alone at home.

Yoav went online and found a local pet store. He ordered a huge basket of all the things that her dog enjoyed. Favorite food, toys etc. and had the name of the dog printed on the basket. He then had a letter attached to the basket addressed to the dog and sent it to corporate headquarters.

Within a few days, Yoav received a call from the CEO of the Fortune 500 company.

Becoming a giftologist is the most powerful way to market whatever you are selling and build a network of people who will do anything for you .

Many companies give gifts to their clients, potential prospects, and staff but they do it all wrong. They usually send crappy little stress balls or pens with the company logo on them.

Nobody cares about your logo.

Nobody cares to receive another baseball cap.

It's meaningless and ends up in a drawer somewhere (if you're lucky),or more likely,in the trash. It's better to send less gifts to less people, but spend the time to get creative and intimate with each gift.

You will create deep, meaningful relationships that will last a lifetime.

When you become a master at giving gifts you will become the most memorable person in your network. The law of reciprocity will play its part and most times (not always) you will receive 100-times what you gave, but don't forget to enjoy the feeling of touching another human being in a powerfully deep way.

Speaking of gifts, after being married for more than 10 years I still haven't managed to get the gift giving thing right with my wife! I guess I need to become a better master at the art of giving gifts. :)

Ask yourself, what makes others memorable to you? Think about someone you had a conversation with that left an impression on you. What was it about them that stood out? Chances are they were extraordinary. Which means they did or said something that was out of the ordinary. We live in a very noisy, busy attention craved world but it also means it's easier to stand out. All you have to do is be a little different.

You Rap?!

In episode 82 of my podcast show I did something different. Something that I don't think any other podcaster has ever done in their intro. I rapped.

Now, i'm a white, British Jew. I should not be rapping. But for some reason I felt like i,t and it came out pretty decent.

In fact, I enjoyed it so much and my guest was so pleasantly surprised that I decided to continue doing a short rap in all my intros. It"s unique. It's quirky. It's memorable.

Of the 300,000 or so podcasts shows out there, mine now has an added ingredient that separates it from all the others. There are so many ways to be a little out of the ordinary.

Almost all the guests I have had on my show have created some way of becoming memorable...

Anil Gupta wears a paper heart on his shirt.

JP Sears wears a headband with a flower in it.

Jon Vroman holds his hands up in a massive V shape.

Joel Comm uses the hashtag #DoGoodStuff.

Stripping Down to Her Underwear on the Streets of NY

Some people go the extra mile when it comes to wanting to become memorable.

Virginia Salas Kastilio stripped down to her underwear and stood blindfolded on the streets of New York asking strangers to draw a heart on her body to support self-acceptance.

She created a massive following on social media, and was named the #1 Female Snapchat Business Influencer in the world, by Inc. Magazine!

Get uncomfortable and start doing something different. Don't worry about people that might look at you funny. Always ask yourself, "How can I remain in the minds of the people I interact with?"

Every day we meet dozens of new people offline and online. Most of them fade away into our subconscious mind lost in the collection of stuff. Leave an impression and remain on the forefront of their mind.

Be remarkable. *Become Memorable.*

Action Step: *The next stranger you interact with do something memorable.*

Be Yourself (everyone else is already taken)

"Always be yourself and have faith in yourself. Do not go out and look for a successful personality and try to duplicate it."

-Bruce Lee

• • • • •

I don't care to beat you.

I race against myself.

I want to better who I am.

I want to be

a better husband,

a better father,

a better businessman,

a better friend,

a better brother,

a better son,

a better human being.

I'm on a single race track.

There is nobody else racing.

There is only me and my better version.

So don't compare yourself to me, because i'm not trying to be better than you.

Stop Idolizing Others

I want you to imagine someone you idolize. It could be your favorite celebrity, sports star or successful entrepreneur. Just picture them in your mind.

Ask yourself this question: *What makes them different to you?*

Honestly, really, ask yourself that question: *What makes them different to you?*

Self-help Addicts tend to look at super achievers and place them on a pedestal. They see them as untouchable and unreachable.

They would never have time for little ole me, they say to themselves.

Successful people look up to other successful people and take the opportunity to get to know them. They aren't afraid of approaching them because they see them as fellow humans and not some unapproachable superpower.

Have you ever watched a celebrity or successful speaker, like Tony Robbins, get on stage? Have you ever stood in the crowd and noticed how the audience is in complete awe of him on that stage?

Watch how they take in every word as if their lives depended on it. They idolize him. They make him their God.

But in reality, he's just a human being with the same vulnerabilities. Speakers get into fights with their loved ones. They get scared. They make financial mistakes. They take a dump.

Have you ever asked the question, "What makes the person on stage so different from me?"

Have you ever asked yourself, "Why am I not on that stage?"

"Why do I see that person as so much greater than me?

The truth is, it's all in your head. The reason why they are on stage and everyone else paid to hear them speak is simply because they got on stage and you bought a ticket.

There is no reason why you can't get on stage, and they buy a ticket to hear you speak.

The difference between Tony and you in that moment is that he's producing and you're consuming.

In this relationship, *he's the producer and you're the consumer.*

The problem is that we limit ourselves. We convince ourselves of a lie. A lie that we have told ourselves over and over again for many years. The lie that we are limited. That we are incapable. That we are not good enough. Not smart enough. Not strong enough.

It's. one. big. fat. lie.

You Already Have Everything You Need

My kids are the best negotiators I know.

My four year old negotiates for "just one more cookie" or "just one more TV show."

I went into a toy store the other day. My boys were like, "Oh, we really want that toy."

I said, "No. That's too expensive."

"But we want that toy."

I said, "Yeah, but that"s a bit pricey. What about this toy?"

Then, they start the negotiation (emotional blackmail) tactics ...

"No daddy, all the kids have this toy." (guilt and social proof)

"No!"

"Please daddy, please!" (persistence)

"No!"

"Oh, daddy. I"ll give you a big hug." (talk to the heart)

"Hmmm"

"I'll do anything you want." (bribery)

"Ummmm..."

"I'll play with my brother. We'll play together." (win-win)

Until eventually I give in ... "Okay. Fine." (deal closed)

My one-and-a-half-year-old starting trying to walk. He lifts himself up, fearlessly grabbing hold of whatever is in front of him. Sometimes he falls and smashes his head on the floor. He cries. Then repeats the same cycle.

Imagine you want to do something but then smashed your head in the process.

How many times would you try before you gave up trying?

Most people would give up after the first few attempts.

But here's the thing. All of us learned how to walk. That process involved smashing our heads, bruising our knees, and bashing our elbows countless times!

What happened to that fearlessness?

What happened to that persistence?

As young children, we were curious, adventurous, courageous, fearless, energized, excited, fascinated, relentless, carefree, and joyous.

What happened?

At some point in our life we started to believe the lies that people told us.

"You can't do that."

"You're not good enough."

"It"s impossible."

"That's not acceptable."

"NO!"

"Better safe than sorry."

"Don't be foolish."

"You should be more like ..."

We believed them, and eventually the external voices became internal voices.

We started talking ourselves out of doing things because we were afraid to fail or look bad.

We went from not caring what others thought of us to hiding behind masks that we thought people wanted to see.

We went from asking for everything we desired to avoiding rejection.

We went from being risk-takers to playing it safe.

My question is at what point in your life did you stop?

What point in your life did you stop being courageous?

You don't need to be courageous. You just need to go back to being courageous.

You already once were courageous. You just stopped.

Something in your life or someone or whatever it was stopped you and you need to claim it back.

What was it that stopped you from being persistent and getting your way because you wanted something?

Why did you stop that? That's the question I want to ask you.

You don't need to look up to anyone to find inspiration. Just look within.

Look at the child you once were.

You went from not being able to say a word to having conversations.

You went from not being able to stand to running, jumping, skipping, and cartwheeling.

You learned skills like reading, writing, playing guitar, drawing, riding a bike, throwing, catching, and swimming.

You don't need anything. You have everything you ever need to accomplish anything you want. And it's within you. It's always been there and it always will be.

You just need to reconnect with it.

Action Step: *Ask your parents what you were like as a child. Watch videos of when you were a child. Notice how adventurous, mischievous, brave, courageous you were. Keep a picture of you as a toddler with you, and look at it when you need a reminder.*

Create a Nation

Find Your 1000 True Fans

The most valuable of all capital is that invested in human beings

- Alfred Marshall

● ● ● ● ●

One day, I stumbled upon an article that would completely revolutionize how I would think about marketing and growing businesses.

The article was written by Kevin Kelly and it was titled "1000 True Fans."

The basic idea is this. To be successful you don't need millions of followers (nor does having millions of followers mean you will be successful). What you really need is 1000 True Fans.

A "True Fan" is someone who buys into what you do.

A "True Fan" will travel a far distance to hear you speak.

A "True Fan" will buy a product or service that you endorse.

A "True Fan" is someone that talks about you to their friends.

A "True Fan" is someone that will pre-order your book before it comes out.

A "True Fan" is someone that looks forward to receiving content you create.

A "True Fan" is someone that becomes an ambassador to what you do and shares it with others.

Numbers are worthless. Real relationships are valuable.

Having thousands of "friends" on Facebook or followers on Twitter and Instagram is worthless. The question is how many of them are True Fans?

True Fans will support you emotionally when times are rough.

True Fans will show up when you need them to.

True Fans will put money in your bank account.

Most importantly, your True Fans will give you the motivation to keep doing what you believe in.

A Personal Army

I recently saw the power of having True Fans.

There was an under 35 entrepreneur summit that was limited to 35 of some of the most influential entrepreneurs under the age of 35. I really wanted to speak at the summit, but there were only a few spaces left. When I reached out to the organiser I was told that it's already booked out. I knew that it was a nice way of saying, "You're not popular enough."

Being one to never give up, I posted on my Facebook page the following "Hey, peeps please comment (click the link) if you want to hear me speak ... Thanks!"

The link went to the organiser's Facebook page. Within minutes of me posting it, dozens of people started commenting on his Facebook page. Here are a few of them ...

"For sure, get Gefen on the summit!"

"Daniel Gefen is tearing it up!!!"

"Daniel Gefen would make a great speaker"

"Daniel Gefen has broad range appeal that will resonate with any audience"

"I'm a big fan of Daniel Gefen"s podcast. He has a good way with people, and he really brings out the best in his podcast guests."

"Daniel Gefen is a serial entrepreneur that is helping others get on board and learn how to do it for themselves. i usually hear him interviewing others but would love to have him on the other side of the mic!"

"I noticed that a lot of people have written Daniel Gefen... I too can without a doubt back them up on this one.... I Love listening to intelligent podcasts and I never get bored of his (hence why he is also a Facebook friend now) he has many ideas and is always able to at least try putting them into action with continuous effort until he gets the desired result! I have heard him speak live before and kept everything relevant and interesting which nowhere near enough speakers do! You can always tell he is willing to learn what he does not know and beyond all he is an Entrepreneur in every sense of the word!"

"If it's not obvious by now...Daniel Gefen"

He didn't know what hit him.

Nor did I.

I was stunned.

I was touched.

The organiser sent me the following message ...

"Hey man! Let's talk soon. I have been swamped by the amount of work but I have to say - your level of dedication amazes me ... (And you have awesome friends?)"

This was a huge lesson for me. When you discover your True Fans make sure you focus on giving them incredible value.

Your True Fans are the most valuable asset you have (besides time).

I decided to create a list of my 1000 True Fans and update it on a daily basis. I simply asked people if they were a True Fan and if they said yes I would add them to my email list. You can imagine how much more responsive my email list is compared to most people who just dump emails in their list and hope for the best.

My network is my secret weapon.

I know that if I publish a book, launch a new product, or create an event, I will get a powerful response.

Remember this: *In a world where most people chase the masses become the person that builds real relationships.*

Go and discover your 1000 True Fans.

Never Underestimate the Power of Social Capital

The cover for this book was designed in exchange for exposure.
(Thanks Jacob Schwartz)

The editing of this book was done in exchange for consulting services.
(Thank you 'anonymous')

The publishing of this book was done in exchange for podcasting services.
(Thanks John North)

The photoshoot of me for the book cover was done in exchange for exposure.
(Thanks Brian Spector)

Someone on in my network reached out and designed the logo for Gefen Media Group.
(Thanks Dan Gepner)

It saved me over $30,000!
Never underestimate the value of social capital!

The People Have Spoken.

Having a large network of engaging fans has another huge benefit. When I want to know what hundreds of people think about something I simply post it on Facebook and within minutes I start getting feedback. It's magical.

For example, when I was deciding on the best cover design for this book I posted my top three choices on Facebook. Within the hour, I had over 60 comments!

I gave a choice of A, B or C. My preference was "A" and I thought that"s what everyone else would say but over 90% voted for "C". I was pleasantly surprised. The people had spoken.

I was once stuck trying to pick a title for one of my podcast episodes so I turned to my Facebook network. I gave them three options. The response was incredible!

Comments were flying in ...

I realised how powerful a network can be.

The secret is that people love to give their opinion. So let them!

Now for every episode I publish, I let my network choose the best title.

I get to use a title that is most likely going to catch my listeners attention.

Most people think they know what people want. Boy, can I tell you how wrong I was so many times! I have lost count how many times I thought people would vote for "A" and they voted for "B."

When the people have spoken, *listen.*

People like to feel involved, and when they do they are more committed.

This is HUGE!

The reason why so many companies run competitions is for this very reason. When you feel part of something, you are way more likely to become committed to that brand or cause.

Imagine if you chose the cover of this book or the title, would you not feel more of an attachment to it? Wouldn't you be more compelled to buy it? Wouldn't you be more likely to talk about it with your network?

The power of involving your network in what you do cannot be overestimated.

Never underestimate the value of social capital!

Action Steps: *Start discovering your 1,000 True Fans. Go on your social media, and ask who considers themselves as a true fan of yours. create an excel spreadsheet and keep adding to the list until you hit 1,000.*

Become a Super Connector

"You can have everything in life you want, if you will just help enough other people get what they want"

– Zig Ziglar

● ● ● ● ●

One of the most memorable guests I have had on my show was a guy named Walter O'Brien.

He's known to be one of the smartest men alive with an IQ of 197! He had an incredible story (to say the least). In fact, he hacked into NASA when he was 13 years old! (Episode 53)

I always wondered if having a genius hacker in my network would come in handy one day.

Not long after I did the interview, I noticed a post on Facebook from my friend Cameron Herold.

He had just got hacked and the hacker was threatening to steal his identity unless he paid a hefty sum of money. I immediately sent Cameron an email introducing him to Walter.

All I said was "Cameron meet Walter. Walter works for the US government, Homeland Security, the FBI, and private clients who have been hacked. You are in good hands …"

They connected and hit it off. They're now really good friends, and Cameron no longer is a hostage to some sleazy slimeball hacker.

It's amazing how easy it is to connect two people, and yet the benefits are huge.

Every time you connect two people, you create a more powerful relationship with each of them.

Think of the last time someone made an introduction to you or on your behalf. It may have been a potential client for your business, a potential partner, or a product or service that benefited you.

How did you feel about that person?

Most likely you felt touched that they thought of you.

How likely are you to recommend them to others? How likely are you to do business with them at some point in the future?

The world is filled with people who focus on themselves and are always asking for things.

When you become the person who focuses on connecting others and providing value to others, you become remarkable.

The more you connect people the more you expand your network. The bigger your network the more opportunities to connect more people. It"s a snowball effect.

There is something truly magical about connecting two people with similar goals that haven't yet crossed paths.

You become someone that people want to be around.

You become someone people want to work with and build a relationship with.

You become an asset.

You become the puzzle piece in their life.

You become the creator of a whole new relationship.

You become the composer of a symphony with endless opportunities and possibilities.

You become a *super connector.*

Remember: *"Your network is your networth."*

Find Canvases for Other People to Paint On

The term "*canvas strategy*" was coined by Ryan Holiday and included as a chapter in Tim Ferriss's book "Tools of Titans."

Here"s a quote from the Ryan explaining what it is:

"That's what the Canvas Strategy is about- helping yourself by helping others. Making a concerted effort to trade your short term gratification for a longer term payoff. Whereas everyone else wants to get credit and be "respected," you can forget credit. You can forget it so hard that you're glad when others get it instead of you, that was your aim, after all. Let the others take their credit on credit, while you defer and earn interest on the principal."

It's by far the most effective way to build your network and open endless doors of opportunity. Period.

Being a "Sucker" Is the Smartest Thing You Can Do in Business

Hillel Fuld is a good friend of mine and one of (if not the) most connected guy in the Israel tech space.

He wrote an article on his blog titled "Being a 'Sucker' Is the Smartest Thing You Can Do in Business. It Built my Career!"

In the article, he explains how 90 percent of his time is not monetized.

Over the past ten years he has written thousands of articles, attended thousands of meetings with startups seeking advice, and helped raise millions of dollars of funding for companies. All for FREE.

He has also connected over a hundred people looking for jobs with companies looking to hire.

How much does he charge? Zero!

I did the math. If he would have charged what a typical recruitment agency charges, he would have pocketed over a million dollars in fees.

So why not charge?

Besides for the fact that he is genuinely a really nice guy, he also sees the long term value in building relationships.

Hillel is a master at the canvas strategy. He patiently creates canvases for others to paint on.

And because of his "give first, receive later" approach he has built himself an incredibly valuable network, has had breakfast with the founder of Apple (he shares that crazy story on my show - episode 5), owns shares in some major tech companies, and has essentially built a venture capital firm without writing a single check.

How to Become the Most Connected Person in the Room

Jayson Gaignard shared how he walked away from a seven-figure business because he valued relationships more than money (episode 115).

He shared a crazy story of how he bought four thousand copies of Tim Ferriss's book to get him to speak at his first-ever conference! At the time, he was a quarter of a million dollars in debt, and had to borrow the money.

He believed in his mission so much that he was willing to do whatever it took.

It paid off.

Today, he is one of the most connected guys on the planet!

His invitation only mastermind talks conference has a lower acceptance rate than Harvard and speakers have included Tim Ferriss, James Altucher, Guy Kawasaki, and Gary Vaynerchuk to name a few.

Rejected to Super Connected

Jon Levy went from being the kid in school that nobody wanted to sit next to, to becoming the man that the biggest influencers and celebrities want to sit with.

The pain of rejection pushed him on a mission to find out how human beings tick. How they make decisions and why they do what they do.

This fascination led him on crazy adventures, from inviting well-known actors and billionaires to dinner to being crushed by a bull after slapping it on the behind (episode 68)!

Jon started inviting "strangers" to dinner but there were some interesting rules he set

- The guest list is kept secret.
- Guests do not know one another beforehand.
- Guests are asked not to discuss their work or achievements.
- All attendees help prepare a simple meal where no cooking experience is necessary.
- Once seated at the dinner table, all attendees take turns guessing what fellow guest"s professions.
- The expense of the meal is covered by the host

As you can imagine, Jon has increased his network dramatically and has also facilitated others to increase their network. Jon became a super connector by creating a platform for others.

Find a platform that works for you. Go out and connect the people in your world.

Become the most connected guy in the room.

Action Step: *Start connecting people. Look for opportunities to make introductions.*

Successful Creators

"The only way to find your voice is to use it"

- Austin Kleon

● ● ● ● ●

You are never truly ready to become a successful creator. You just *become* one.

I was never ready to become a podcast host. *I just started interviewing people.*

I was never ready to become a published author. *I just started writing.*

I was never ready to become a husband. *I just put a ring on her finger and committed to loving her forever.*

I was never ready to become a father. *I just held my first child in my arms and knew I would do whatever it takes to provide for him.*

You might prefer writing; you may find speaking to be more natural. Maybe video is your thing.

I love speaking. It's what comes most natural. After speaking, writing is my next most powerful tool. I don't love being in front of the camera but that can easily change after doing enough Facebook lives.

The key is to start with what comes most natural to you. If you don't think you are good at any of them then just start with what is least uncomfortable.

The goal is to master your craft. With enough consistency, I guarantee that you will become a master at one of them.

This is your way of communicating.

This is how you will be able to find your voice, share your story with your world, create your movement, and leave your legacy.

Through the power of speech, I am able to get on stages and share what I'm passionate about. I'm able to transform lives and make an impact on the world around me. I'm able to negotiate business deals and provide for my family. I'm able to share my deepest feelings with my loved ones.

Though the power of writing I am able to write this book, which you hold in your hands. I can craft powerful sales copy that gets people to buy my services. I'm able to construct persuasive emails that get people to take action. I can write a heartfelt text to my wife.

Video is a very powerful way to create a deeper connection with your followers as they can see what you look like. Humans crave human interaction especially in the digital world where everyone is hiding behind bits of text and branding.

These are all forms of art. To become a successful creator, you must *become an artist.* You must master the art of communicating. Once you become the master of communication, your opportunities will become endless. You will be able to earn as much as you want, build strong relationships, and even save lives.

The list of things you can produce are endless but here are some of my favorite and most powerful ways to become a Successful Creator.

If speaking is your most natural instrument then you could:
- Start a podcast show
- Be a guest on podcasts
- Start getting free speaking gigs

If writing is more your thing then:
- Start writing a book
- Start a daily blog
- Start writing for online publications

If you're not camera shy then:
- Start a daily Vlog on your YouTube channel
- Start recording daily Facebook Lives
- Start doing daily Instagram videos

Addictions are hard to break. Self-help Addicts spend many years procrastinating and over analyzing things. The only way to break the cycle is to produce on a consistent basis.

Successful Creators produce regularly. Whether it's writing an article or a page in their new book. Recording a podcast episode or appearing as a guest on a show. Recording a Facebook Live video or producing their daily vlog.

Successful Creators are Constantly Creating.

Gary Vaynerchuk started out working for his father in his liquor store and grew it from $3 million to $60 million by producing a daily video on YouTube where he tasted wines and demystified the wine market for the average casual wine drinker. His videos were viewed over 100,000 times!

Today, he consistently produces two daily vlogs. "The Daily Vee" is where he documents and shows you the behind the scenes of his day-to-day schedule, and the "Ask Gary Vee Show" where he (and sometimes a special guest) answers questions from his followers.

His consistent producing has paid off massively. He now runs a media agency called Vaynermedia, which currently does around $100 million in annual revenue

He also gets paid up to $100,000 as a keynote speaker!

Casey Neistat started a daily vlog just documenting himself doing ridiculous things like chasing a police car on his bike or snowboarding with the NYPD, and amassed an audience of 5 million subscribers. His videos have been viewed more than a billion times!

He"s a high school dropout turned self-made media celebrity by consistently producing a daily video.

John Lee Dumas started a daily podcast show 7 days a week called "Entrepreneur On Fire" and to date has produced over 1700 episodes which generates him a monthly income of around $200,000!

Seth Godin writes on a daily basis.

He has written 18 books and more than 2,500 blog posts. As a result, he has amassed a huge following, and is a highly sought-after speaker and marketing consultant.

Gary Vaynerchuk and Casey Neistat love to be in front of the camera. John Lee Dumas uses the mic as his secret weapon and Seth Godin makes magic with his keyboard but the one thing they all have in common is that they produce EVERY. SINGLE. DAY.

They have mastered their art through the power of consistently creating.

Successful Creators are not born. They are produced.

Action Steps: *Find your platform and start performing.*

Write Your Own Book

A day will come when the story inside you will want to breathe on its own.

That's when you'll start writing.

- Sarah Noffke

● ● ● ● ●

I get asked a lot what my favorite book is. My answer usually pleasantly surprises them.

My favorite book is *the one I publish.*

Why did I write this book? There are a number of reasons.

The main reason I wrote this book is because it was the one thing I procrastinated the most about.

I remember sitting in a therapist's chair around six years ago telling her that I really wanted to write a book called The Self-help Addict.

She asked why I hadn't written it yet. I said it was because I was a perfectionist, and I needed the book to be perfect. (Ironically, I needed to read the book I wanted to write in order to write it!)

Why should YOU write a book?

Here are a few reasons...

Identity

Because as Self-help Addicts we consume so many ideas from other thought leaders, we struggle with our own identity. We struggle with the question of "Who am I?"

A leader is someone who has a strong identity and is able to stand for something they believe in. They are able to clearly express who they are, and what they believe in. They have a strong sense of purpose. They surround themselves with others who align with their beliefs and values.

One of the most effective ways to discover your true identity is to write. I have no idea how it works but for some reason when you write you tap into your subconscious, you enter into some kind of hypnotic state. It's one of the best forms of therapy in my opinion.

Self-expression

As Self-help Addicts, we find it hard to express ourselves. We get frustrated because we want so desperately to share our ideas with others, but don't know where to begin. We struggle with putting it all into words on paper.

Essentially, we don't know how to bring down the infinite into the world of the finite. We live in the world of the abstract, which is fine for short periods of time, but we want to enter the world of concrete existence.

When you write, you are taking your ideas and bringing them into reality.

You are transferring potential into actual. You are shaping your ideas and giving them form. You are creating a vessel that can be used to pass on your knowledge and experience to others.

I have a message I am passionate about and want to share with others.

I know that as an author, I will have a key that will open doors that are closed unless you are a published author.

I will get invited to speak at events.

I will be presented with new business opportunities.

Pride

I can't tell you how proud I am when I look back at all the pages I have written. I feel an incredible sense of accomplishment. It's not coming from a place of ego but rather from a place of deep self worth.

Like anything you struggle to do and then finally overcome, you feel incredible once you finally give birth to your first book.

The feeling of holding your book for the first time is literally akin to holding your own child for the first time. (I know it sounds a little insane.) Your child is someone who will continue your legacy. So to your book will continue your legacy long after you have left this world.

The day you publish your book will be one of the proudest moments of your life.

Document your life

Sometimes I look back at things I have written years ago, and it's like I'm reading something my son wrote.

I can see myself maturing through the years of writing. I can laugh at strange ideas I once had. I can recognize how much my viewpoints and opinions have changed over time. I can remember moments that were lost in the messy attic of my mind. Some happy moments. Some sad. Some scary and some exciting.

Money comes and goes but memories last forever.

The most powerful business card

Damian Mark Smyth is a good friend of mine and also happens to be one of the people who gave me the kick up the ass I needed to finish this book. He was once on a flight, and the person sitting next to him asked what he did for a living. Damian smiled and pulled out a copy of his book "Do Nothing", handed it to him, and said, "Read that and it will tell you everything about me."

After a couple of hours, the guy turns to Damian and says, "That was incredible. I need to hire you!"

Business cards are like junk mail. They get tossed in the trash within moments of arriving in the recipient"s hands. When was the last time you kept someone's business card?

Imagine the next networking event you attend, instead of handing out a business card like everyone else, you hand out copies of your book. It's definitely less likely to end up in the trash and there's a very good chance you will end up finding a permanent home in someone's office or living room. Now that's powerful.

The key to many doors

Being a published author automatically enters you into an exclusive club.

It's amazing how many doors fly open once you become a published author.

Speaking invitations, business opportunities, Partnerships, joint ventures, jobs, consulting gigs, press and media, podcast appearances etc.

Earn more

You are perceived as an expert in your field, which allows you to charge higher fees as a consultant. You can charge more for your product or service because people are willing to pay more for a company that is positioned as the leader in the market.

Free press

You are seen as a trusted advisor and are asked to be quoted in industry or topic specific publications.

You are more likely to get media appearances as an author.

The best gift you could give your grandchildren

In the introduction to this book, I wrote a message to my eldest son, Elisha.

One day he will read this book and it will be worth more to him than all the money in the world.

One of the most powerful motivators for writing this book is that I will have something I can pass on to my children and future generations.

Imagine if I told you that your great grandfather wrote a book. Would you want to read it?

You bet you would! I would pay a lot of money if someone told me they had a copy of a book my great-grandfather wrote.

Stop Being Selfish

I actually think you are selfish if you don't write a book. You are depriving your children and grandchildren from having something they can cherish for years after you leave this world.

You're holding it back from everybody else. You could be inspiring so many people, your grandchildren, your great-grandchildren, years to come after you pass away. They can have something that you created, that you produced in your lifetime. If you don't produce it, you're selfish. You're holding it back from them. Don't do that. If you can't do it for yourself do it for them.

Don't go to your grave with your book buried inside you.

"But what can I write about?"

I can hear you ask.

ANYTHING

Just start writing.

I'm serious. If you just start writing on a daily basis you will find that you have more to talk about than you thought you did. In fact you will actually discover a whole new world inside of you you never knew existed.

It can take time to get into the flow (sometimes, I can sit staring at white space for eternity until I start typing) but when you do it's magical.

I can't tell you the amount of times I have read something I wrote months later and said to myself "Did I really write that?"

It's almost as if I am reading someone else's writing.

Writing is an art. There is no right or wrong way to do it. Everyone has their own unique style. That's what's so incredible about it.

Think of all the books that have been written on the subject of time management. How can there be so many books published on the same subject?

The answer is that different people enjoy different styles of writing.

There are probably thousands of books written on the subject of marketing but I find most of them boring. I really love reading books written by Seth Godin. I like his style of writing. Some people may not like him and prefer other authors.

The point is that the people who will buy your book will be the people that like your style of writing. The stories you tell. The tone you "speak" in. The ideas you share. The way you structure your sentences. The titles and subtitles you choose. Your sense of humour. Your strong viewpoints. Your personal story. The parables and examples you use. Your style of language. Your honesty. Your choice of words.

Some people will read this book and put it down after reading a chapter. Some will read till the end and want to read more.

I don't need to write a book that speaks to everyone. I just need to write a book. Period.

If just one person reads this book and makes just one positive change in their life as a result then it made it all worth the while. Even if that one person is me.

Helpful Tips

Here are some things that helped me when writing my book:

Music

I don't know what it is, but there is something very powerful about music. I spend a lot of time listening to inspirational music when I work. In fact, as I'm writing this sentence I am listening to a two-hour mix of epic Celtic music on YouTube.

It's amazing how much more productive I am when I put on my headphones, and get lost in the hypnotic state of the music I'm listening to. It literally drowns out everything else around me and allows me to just focus intently on what I'm doing.

In fact, when I was younger I used to visit the dentist regularly (too much candy, too little brushing) I hated the sound of the drilling so I plugged in my earphones and listened to Celine Dion full blast (that's my little secret so don't tell anyone!)

Fast, pumped up music is great when I want to smash out some things fast like a bunch of emails. Classical music is great when I need a winding down at the end of the day, and inspirational music is perfect for when I want to get creative and feel inspired.

You can change your energy levels in minutes. For example, if I'm feeling a bit slow or sluggish (usually on a Monday morning) I will get pumped up to some high-paced rock songs. When I'm feeling way too energetic, and need to calm down because I'm jumping all over the place, I calm down to some jazz.

Music affects your emotions. Different types of music elicit different reactions.

With the power of music you can gain instant access to any state of mind you desire.

Powerful stuff indeed.

Environment

Find a quiet place where you won't be distracted by anyone. If you can't find a quiet place to be then use headphones.

Time of day

Some people find that mornings are the best time to focus and be creative while others prefer nighttime. Usually, the two ends of the day are when we are at our most creative, probably because that's when the world is quiet.

Find the best time for you and make that the time you write.

Block out time

As I'm writing this book, I am sitting in the business lounge of the hotel we are staying at for the summer. My wife and kids are in the pool.

We are here for nine days and I told my wife before we came that I must have time every day to write in my book. We agreed that first thing in the morning after breakfast I would come to the business lounge for two hours to write and she would take the kids to swim.

The rest of the day, i'll spend with them, but I know that if I don't block out these two hours every morning I won't write.

Get into the habit of writing for a period of time every single day. No matter where you are.

If you need any help writing your book head over to www.TheSelfHelpAddict.com/BookLaunch

Action Step: *Start writing your book!*

Launch Your Own Podcast

"Most people I know are interested in on-demand stuff; podcasts are is essentially audio Netflix."

– Jordan Harbinger

● ● ● ● ●

The thought of "What if I didn't start my podcast?" gives me goosebumps.

My podcast has opened so many doors for me.

Including:

- Building an incredibly powerful network
- Creating dozens of strategic partnerships
- Writing a book
- Being invited to speak
- Curating a wealth of knowledge
- Amassing a tribe of loyal followers
- Getting featured in Forbes, INC and other major publications
- Attracting investors, clients and advisors for my company

By far one of the most game-shifting things I have done to advance my business and self-brand was starting a podcast show.

This is what Gary Vaynerchuk had to say about the power of audio:

"Before AR and VR and AI, audio is going to be the next major platform shift for consumer attention. It's here today! What are you going do?

Why do you think I do so many podcasts? Do I really think that the audio shows that I appear on have a million listeners that are going to convert and follow my page? I don't.

Do I think that podcasting is going to have a disproportionately strong impact on my life in the next 1-6 months? I don't. What about 1-2 years? Probably not. But do I think there are going to be 12 people that listen to my podcast or an appearance I've made as a guest on another show who don't know a thing about me that are going to become a fan and like what I do? Absolutely.

Do I think that after the hundreds of appearances I'll make over the next decade, that one of the podcasters starting today is going to become a breakout hit and move on to become a big-time celebrity starting their own company and later want to do business with me? I sure do!

I'm playing the long game, and I'm capitalizing on the medium of the moment. I have a strong feeling that the people who consume my podcasts daily are the techy silicon valley type who want to start a business because they know who I am. I would love for that to play out in 15 years with the next Elon Musk emailing me about an episode or thanking me for the 15 minutes on his or her show. Just remember, audio and voice are by far the most natural interface for humans to interact. We like to speak and listen.

There was roughly 1.5X more audio consumed than video according to Nielsen statistics on streaming in 2016. This is HUGE."

All the big influencers are jumping on podcast shows and there's a good reason for it...

Here are some of the top reasons why:

- **Power of Storytelling** - Podcasts are the best platform to share your story and message with a highly engaged audience.

- **Instant Credibility** - The host chose to have you on as their guest so you must be someone special and trustworthy.

- **Evergreen Content** - With traditional marketing once your ad spend is depleted your leads dry up. With podcast shows, you can get leads for years to come. Gotta love evergreen content!

- **Consumable On The Go** - People can't watch videos or read articles while driving or running but they can listen to a podcast.

- **People Buy from People** - People don't connect to ad banners or promotional content. They connect with real people.

- **High Level of Engagement** - People who listen to podcasts are highly engaged and focused on listening to what is being said. You literally have the audience in the palm of your hand.

- **Highly Targeted** - Podcasts are categorized and usually consist of a clearly defined focused audience.

Your Network is Your Networth

Today, the most effective and quickest way to network with the most influential people is to launch a podcast.

My podcast has allowed me to speak one on one with the smartest man alive (Walter O'Brien), a leading FBI hostage negotiator (Chris Voss), a billionaire (Jeff Hoffman), top influencers like Jayson Gaignard, Tom Bilyeu, Noah Kagan, Peter Shankman and Alex Charfen; leading marketing experts including Jay Abraham, Yanik Silver and Russell Brunson; the leading social media experts including Sue B Zimmerman, Virginia Salas kastilio and Joel Comm; thought leaders like Verne Harnish, Cameron Herold and Kelsey Ramsden; and celebrities like Matisyahu and JP Sears.

These are just some of the people I have had the fortune to have on my show. Best of all, I have kept in touch with most of them.

After just two years I now have some of the top influencers and leading experts in my personal network.

Without my podcast as a platform to invite them to speak, it would have been much harder and taken way longer to connect with them.

You could probably go to an event where they are speaking and introduce yourself to them. You may get a few minutes of their time. But to get an hour of exclusive time with them won't happen unless you have the money. Jay Abraham charges $25,000 for a one day coaching session, Verne Harnish charges $50,000 for a keynote speech, Gary Vaynerchuk charges $100,000 to speak, but they all go on podcast shows for FREE.

If that's not a great reason to start a podcast I don't know what is!

Cameron Herold was responsible for taking a junk removal company, 1800-Got-Junk, from $6 million in annual revenue to over $100 million in just six years. I had the honor of having Cameron on my show, and after the show, we got chatting. He asked what I was doing besides the podcast. I told him about my new venture Gefen Media Group and he loved the concept.

In fact, he became a major ambassador of the brand!

Cameron has sent us a ton of referrals, and his experience and wisdom has been priceless.

This happened directly because of him becoming a guest on my show.

Build a highly engaged following

There is something psychologically powerful about being in someone's ears. When I read your blog, I connect to you on some level but not nearly as much as when I listen to your voice. Hearing someone's voice creates a strong connection that is unparalleled to when I read what you have written.

As a podcast host, you're following is extremely loyal.

People who listen to podcasts say they feel like they "know" the host on a personal level.

I have had people write to me saying that they listened to my episodes back to back while traveling on a long road trip!

Your podcast can be used as a platform to get people to take further action: sign up to your email list, join your Facebook group, check out your blog, buy your products/services, and come to your event.

People can consume your content wherever they go, whatever they're doing.

Going for a jog, driving to work, doing the dishes, gardening, working out, folding laundry, climbing a mountain, chilling by the pool. You have their attention when bloggers and YouTubers don't.

Podcasting Myths

I have heard so many excuses for why people have not launched their own podcast.

Here are my responses to them.

"It's too expensive to run a podcast show."

I spend less than $150 a month to run my show!

"It takes too much time to run a podcast."

I spend less than 3 hours per episode!

"You need to be a professional speaker."

I didn't have any speaking experience before starting my show!

"It's too technical."

I am the least techy guy you will meet!

"I have nothing to talk about."

You will be surprised how much more you have to say once you start speaking!

"Finding great guests is so difficult."

I get too many people asking to be a guest on my show!

"I don't know how I will make money from it"

In the short term you won't but in the long run it will become your most valuable asset!

Need help launching your podcast? Head over to www.TheSelfHelpAddict.com/PodcastLaunch

Action Step: *Launch your podcast!*

Transformation

Being and Becoming

I live on a seesaw.

On one side is the need to create, do big things, and make an impact.

On the other is the desire to be, to enjoy what I have, to accept myself as I am.

The seesaw is rarely balanced.

It's either up on one side and down on the other or vice versa.

It's the struggle between *Doing and Being.*

Trying to keep the seesaw balanced is really tough.

But I know that it's the key to real success.

When I originally thought of writing this book I thought I had the cure for a Self-help Addict. It was simple. Just take action. Just become a creator instead of a consumer.

Becoming a super achiever meant producing, creating, doing, leading, inspiring, and motivating. That is to say, it meant becoming.

But as I evolved from a consumer to a producer, I noticed something missing. There was a gaping hole inside me.

I had produced a top-rated podcast show, built a large following of raving fans, built two successful businesses, spoken in front of thousands of people, been featured in major media outlets, and yet I felt empty.

Why?

It didn't make any sense.

The Plague of Emptiness

Why was I still waking up feeling so empty inside?

How could I publish a book about breaking free when I didn't feel freedom?

I can't begin to describe the frustration and confusion that plagued me.

I would look at my wife and four children and feel so blessed yet so depressed.

If I had all this then why did I feel so empty?

And then, one day as I was sitting in a friend's house, and I noticed a book lying on his dining room table. It was a book called "*The Power of Now*" by Eckhart Tolle. I picked up the book and couldn't put it down.

This was the missing piece to my puzzle!

I realised that there are two journeys a Self-help Addict must take. One is becoming a producer — taking action, producing, creating, doing, leading, inspiring, motivating, and becoming.

But the other journey is to just *be* — to learn to live in the moment, accepting yourself without any judgements or conditions. To be present, humble, loving, carefree, lighthearted, childlike, playful, spontaneous, fully aware and abundantly grateful.

This was the missing piece.

I had embarked on a journey of becoming better, stronger, richer, happier, fuller, more popular, more influential. *More. More. More.*

It was like climbing an endless mountain. The more I climbed the more there was to climb. Every time I thought I had reached the top it was just the beginning of a new climb. I was so focused on getting to the top that I wasn't taking in the breathtaking view along the way.

I was missing life.

Life was passing me by as I climbed harder and faster. Less time spent with my children. Less time with my wife. Less time enjoying the food I was eating. Less time enjoying the beautiful sky or the fresh crisp air. Less time being grateful for what I had.

More time at the office. More time building. More time producing. More time reaching. More time climbing.

Once I realized what was happening, I stopped like a runaway train screeching to a sudden halt.

I breathed.

I looked around me and for the first time in a long time, I took in everything.

My beautiful family. My home. My health. The birds in the sky. The leather seats in my car. The flickering of a dancing candle. The smell of my youngest child after a bath. The sound of nature. The sound of silence. The sound of my own breath. The rhythmic beating of my heart.

Try it.

Put down this book.

Look around you.

What do you *see?*

Now, look closer.

What colors pop out?

See the different textures and contrasts.

See the shapes and sizes.

Now *listen*.

What do you hear?

Birds outside?

The ticking of a clock?

The sounds of children playing?

The sound of your own heart beating?

Now *feel*.

Feel the sensations at the tip of your fingers.

Twinkle your toes.

Feel your breath going in and out.

Feel the air surrounding you.

Feel the life energy moving within and around you.

Now *smell*.

Can you smell anything?

Maybe some food.

The crisp air.

A nearby flower.

Fresh laundered clothes.

Now *Taste.*

Pick up the closest food to you and take a bite.

Close your eyes and savor the taste.

Is it sweet?

Is it sour?

Spicy?

Salty?

Fresh?

Crunchy?

Taste the different combinations of ingredients.

Hold onto the aftertaste. Relish it. Enjoy it fully.

Welcome to the moment.

Welcome to timelessness.

Welcome to the only reality that exists.

Welcome back to life.

I stayed in this awakened state for a few weeks. I didn't want it to end. I was finally living. I felt free. I felt alive. Social media no longer had me by my balls. Nobody can take this away from me. I relished every moment. Colors were brighter. Sounds crisper. Smells richer.

But then came the fog.

I suddenly felt confused again.

Something didn't feel right. I had neglected my business. My podcast show. My book. I had found myself a nice private beautiful garden and hid away.

I was broken in two.

On the one hand, I wanted to stay in my garden forever. Just me and my family and friends. Living in bliss. Peace and harmony. In the moment. For the moment. Everlasting happiness.

On the other hand, I felt a need to give. To inspire and produce. To grow and conquer. To plant and provide. To become and be part of.

I swung like a pendulum back and forth between these two states of Being and Becoming.

When I first started writing this book, I wrote about the art of Becoming. Becoming a producer, not a consumer. Becoming a super achiever, not a self-help addict. Becoming the person you dream of becoming. I now realise that this is only half the battle of a self-help addict. The other half is Being.

Like me, you will start to sway like a pendulum back and forth between these two states of Being and Becoming but you need BOTH. One without the other will lead to unfulfillment.

The only way to feel truly whole is to balance these two states.

How?

It isn't easy. It takes time. It takes patience. It takes acceptance. And it takes a lot of self-awareness.

You must understand that *you are completely perfect the way you are.* Period.

No ifs or buts.

Nothing about you needs to change. You were created perfect. Nothing and no one can change that.

Understand this well.

If you truly believe that, then and only then, can you work on growth without feeling down when you fall. And you will fall. Many times. We all do.

When you believe that you are lacking nothing then nothing will get you down.

The only reason we give up is because we feel defeated. You cannot be defeated. Nothing can defeat you. You are unique. Nobody in the history of the world was exactly the same as you and nobody until the end of time will ever be exactly like you.

Your uniqueness, your collective self, your core being is unbreakable.

Striving for more is not a contradiction. We were placed on this earth to produce. You were put here for a unique purpose. Only you can fulfill that unique purpose. You were created to be and become. You are on a mission to conquer yet you are also on a mission to accept.

Count your blessings but never get complacent.

Enjoy the view and keep climbing the mountain.

Loving What Is and What Will Be

I love my one-year-old. He's so adorable. I love the way he wobbles as he takes his first steps. I love the way he makes sounds as he tries to say a word. I love how he curls up in a ball to sleep. He's so innocent and vulnerable.

But would I want him to remain as he is forever?

Would I want him to never grow up?

Would I want to freeze him in this state so I can enjoy him at this age until I die?

No way!

I want to watch him grow. I want to attend his school plays. I want to be there for him when he has his first fight. I want to walk him down his wedding aisle. I want to hold his children. I want to talk to him, train with him and guide him through life.

Is he perfect right now? You bet! He couldn't be more perfect. And as each day goes by and he grows a little more. He takes another step. He says a word. He goes to the bathroom by himself. He answers me back. He becomes independent. I will love him more and more.

Just as you love a child and you could never imagine loving them more. Just like you can never imagine them being more perfect than they already are. So too, you must love yourself and see yourself as absolutely perfect just the way you are. But that shouldn't stop you from growing. There is no contradiction. It is the paradox of life.

We love and we love even more. We see perfection and then we perfect ourselves even more. We lack nothing and strive for everything at the same time. Life is timeless and yet it's bound by time.

The world is perfect and yet everything evolves.

The balance between Being and Becoming is to love yourself so much that you want to see yourself grow.

You want to achieve more because you can. You want to inspire others because you can. You live in the moment and yet the future is the potential for more incredible moments.

You embrace change while simultaneously cherishing the present state.

You fall in love with yourself each step of the journey.

It's All About The Journey

There is no finish line. There is no end. It's all about the journey. The adventure. The experience.

Life is an experiment. We learn and strive to do better. If you don't enjoy the journey you will live a miserable life. Because life is the journey. Stop chasing the promise land and recognize that the moment is an end in itself. This moment contains all of life. Your life is just a collection of millions of moments.

Self-help addicts fall into a depressed state because they focus on having instead of being. Things come and go. Money, property, status, fame, people, come and go. Experiences last forever. You can lose everything but you can't lose your experiences. You can be robbed of everything you have. But nobody can take away your experiences. The more you chase something the further away it seems. It is when you let go of chasing the goal that you actually start to achieve it. You start to enjoy the process and the progress. You no longer need the prize.

The journey becomes sweeter than the destination.

Action Step: *Practice having your feet on both sides of the seesaw.*

The Power Of Silence

One day an old farmer decided to clear out his barn. It was a complete mess and hadn't been organised in years.

He started clearing out all the old junk and animal waste. He collected all the hay and piled them into neatly packed bundles. Then he swept the floor and wiped the windows clean till they sparkled in the glistening sun. He swept the floor and for the first time in what seemed like forever, he could actually move around easily without falling over things.

He then looked up and noticed the roof needed fixing so he climbed up a ladder and filled in some gaps where the rain had created cracks. The sun was baking down and he was sweating profusely, but he barely noticed as he diligently worked throughout the day to make his barn pristine again.

Shortly before sunset, he finally emerged from the barn wiping his brow. He stood there for a few moments proud of his work.

As he was about to head home for some well-deserved dinner, he looked down at his wrist to check the time. He almost fainted.

His watch that was passed down to him from his grandfather was missing!

He quickly ran back into the barn in search of his priceless possession.

As his heart raced he started throwing hay all over the place in desperation.

The Self Help Addict

After half an hour of turning his barn upside down, he was left hopeless. Now his barn looked worse than before but he didn't care. He would do anything to find his precious memorabilia.

Suddenly, he heard a group of children playing outside. He ran out and shouted "Whoever can find my watch will get a nickel!"

The group of young boys raced into the barn throwing themselves in all directions scrambling to find it. As the sun set and the boys grew tired and weary, they came out empty handed.

The old farmer was downtrodden.

As he was heading home he felt a tug on his shirt. He turned around to face a little boy.

"Please sir. I can find your watch for you." He said in a quiet voice.

"Go home boy," said the old farmer. "It's dark now and several boys have already tried searching for it an hour in the daylight to no avail."

The boy was shy but stubborn.

"Please sir. Give me 5 minutes. I promise if I don't find it I will go home."

The farmer nodded hesitantly.

The little boy quickly disappeared into the barn.

Time stood on end.

After just a minute the boy emerged from the barn with a smile from ear to ear. In his tiny hand dangled an old watch.

The farmer couldn't believe his eyes. "But how did you find it in the dark in such a short period of time?" He asked in complete surprise.

"Simple!" The boy said. "All I did was sit on the floor in the middle of the barn and stayed silent until I could hear the ticking of the watch."

Sometimes all we need to do is *stop and listen.*

Action Step: *Shhhhhhhhh*

Lefkowitz and Feldman

One of my favorite stories is a true story about a man called Mr Lefkowitz. Lefkowitz was a wealthy old man that unfortunately lost his ability to walk and became confined to a wheelchair.

He was one of those guys that was always filled with joy even when he had good reason to be down in the dumps.

Lefkowitz had his own room in a home for the elderly as he could afford to pay extra.

One day a nurse approached him and said,

"Mr lefkowitz, all the rooms in the home are full and there is someone who needs a room. Do you mind if he shares your room just for a short while as we try to find him a place?"

Without hesitation, Lefkowitz says "SURE!"

Later that day a tall elderly man with a downcast face moves in.

Lefkowitz wheels himself over and sticks out his hand with a big smile to introduce himself, "Hi my name is Joshuah Lefkowitz but you can call me Lefky for short!"

"My name is Mr Feldman," came the response ... "I don't want to be here and I have no interest in talking to you."

Lefkowitz felt a little taken back but promptly wheeled himself over to his side of the room to give his new roommate some space.

After a few minutes, Lefkowitz wheeled himself over to the other side of the room in another attempt to welcome his new 'guest'. He was stopped in his tracks.

"Listen..." Feldman growled, "I don't want to speak to you. I don't want to be here but I have no choice. I lost my eyesight and now I can't see my own children or grandchildren. I'm just an old blind guy getting ready to die. So please do me a favour and just leave me alone."

Lefkowitz was speechless. He got the message loud and clear and soberingly wheeled himself back to his bed.

A few hours passed and Lefkowitz suddenly became very excited. He quickly wheeled himself over to Feldman and said "Hey Feldman, I know you don't want to be here and I know you don't want to speak to me, but I just had a crazy idea. You are blind and I am confined to a wheelchair. Why don't you put me on your shoulders and I will tell you where to go. I will be your eyes and you will be my legs! We can run around and make entertain everyone..."

"That's a dumb idea!" grumbled Feldman. "I told you to leave me alone!"

Lefkowitz didn't give up. "OK, Feldman. Fine. I understand you're not in the mood right now. But I want to let you know that starting from tomorrow morning, I am going to go over to the window in the room and describe to you what I see outside. You may not wish to be my legs but I will become your eyes."

The next morning, as promised, Lefkowitz called out to Feldman: "Good morning, Feldman!"

He proceeded to describe the beautiful sunrise in great detail.

Feldman sat up and listened intently as Lefkowitz went on to describe the colour of the leaves on the trees, the children getting on the school bus, the dog chasing the cat ...

Days turned into weeks. Weeks turned into months. Feldman would sit enthralled and spellbound each day as Lefkowitz would take him on a mental walk outside and paint a picture in his mind of all the wonderful things life presented outside of their window.

Feldman and Lefkowitz became close friends and one day Feldman says "Hey Lefky, you know that crazy idea you had about me being your legs ... hop on board!"

Feldman ran around with Lefky on his shoulders shouting out the directions, barely missing near collisions with all sorts of things. They were laughing and giggling like little boys.

One night Feldman called out to Lefky, "Hey Lefky, I wanna tell you something ... Most of my life I had perfect vision but could never really see the world for it's true beauty. Over the last few months as a blind old man, I have been fortunate enough to finally see for the very first time and it's thanks to you. I cannot thank you enough, my friend."

The next morning Feldman woke up startled. Something wasn't right. What time was it? Did Lefky sleep in? I didn't hear the sunrise ...

"Lefky, wake up!" No response.

"Lefky... what happened to sunrise? What's happening outside? ...Lefky?" No response.

Feldman quickly called for the nurse.

The nurse came rushing in. "Is everything alright, Mr Feldman?"

"No. Can you please wake Lefkowitz up. He overslept!"

The nurse stood in silence for a moment.

"I'm really sorry Mr Feldman, but Mr Lefkowitz passed away last night of a heart attack."

With tears welling up in eyes, Feldman asked: "What time is the funeral? I want to be there for him."

"I will let you know and arrange for someone to take you," replied the nurse.

As the nurse was turning to leave Feldman called out to her "Before you leave, can you do me a favor?"

"What is it?"

"Lefky used to tell me what was going on outside the window. Can you go over to the window and tell me what's happening right now?"

The nurse replied with confusion: "I'm sorry Mr Feldman. I'm not sure what you mean. There are no windows in this room."

"What do you mean there are no windows!" Yelled Feldman while he scattered out of his bed onto the floor. "There must be a window! Lefkowitz described the schoolchildren, the busses, the trees, the crazy dogs, the sunsets..." Feldman thrust his hands to touch the walls surrounding him. Making his way around the room. His hands desperately trying to find the window.

But all he could find was walls.

Lefkowitz had created a window where there was a wall.

Sometimes we meet people who are surrounded by walls.

They can't see past the walls that hold them prison to the true beauty of life around them.

Go and create windows.

Action Step: *Look for walls to convert into windows.*

Your Roots Are Your Foundation

Live as though all your ancestors were living again through you.

• • • •

There was once a leaf that complained that it was attached to a tree.

It felt restricted and wanted to escape.

It looked up at the birds flying around freely and wished to be like them.

One day a big gust of wind came and the leaf got its wish. It became detached from the tree and started to fly.

As it floated in the sky, it felt so happy and relieved to be finally free.

Then the wind stopped.

The leaf slowly descended down until it lay helpless on the ground.

As it started to wither and die, it looked up at the tree and realised that it was the tree that gave it life. Being attached to the tree is what kept the leaf alive.

Freedom isn't becoming more detached, but rather becoming more connected.

My Greatest Inspiration

If you were to ask me who the person I look up to the most is, I would say, without hesitation, my grandfather.

I've interviewed over 100 super achievers. Not one of them comes close to inspiring me as much as my grandfather.

When he was 14 years old he was in Auschwitz (among dozens of other camps). He watched both of his parents get shot in the head.

He watched all of his siblings slaughtered.

When the Nazis were firing bullets, one of the bullets hit him in the shoulder and he fell to the ground. He stayed down because he knew that if he'd get up again, the next bullet would hit him in the head. He stayed down until it got dark pretending to be dead amongst all the bodies and then when he thought it was safe, he climbed out. He ran into the woods but they found him and they decided to hang him.

While the noose was around his neck and they were about to end his life, the sirens went off and he managed to escape. It was a false alarm. They thought the Russians were coming.

He ran into the forest. They chased him down. They caught him. They hung him up again.

The noose was around his neck and then for the second time the sirens went off. Another false alarm. My grandfather managed to escape again.

On another occasion, he was about 15 feet from the gas chambers. He was standing in line and a Nazi soldier was standing next to him. There was a horse next to the Nazi and it defecated on the Nazi's boot. He turned around to my grandfather who was standing next to him and he said, "You, dirty Jew, come over here and clean my boot." My grandfather got on his hands and knees and cleaned up the boot. When he finished cleaning it, he said to my grandfather, "Get out of here."

My grandfather was saved by horse excrement.

He was the only survivor in his whole family. He had lost everything. When I say everything, I mean *everything*. When he was liberated he had to start from scratch. He had nothing. No contacts, no family, no material possessions, not a penny to his name.

But he didn't despair. He rebuilt himself. He built a family. He built a business. He became part of a community. He gave a lot of charity. And he always smiled.

If you want to know what success means to me, *that* is success, because *he had every reason to give up*. He had every reason to take his own life on so many occasions. Nobody would have blamed him for doing so.

But he didn't.

He believed that there was something worth living for.

He needed to keep going. He needed to produce. He needed to keep moving forward. He needed to continue fighting for what he believed in. He saw the bigger picture and because of him, I am alive today.

The moment of truth

You know when you are on your way to the airport to catch a flight and you have that unsettled feeling that you may have forgotten something? That's how I feel right now.

The thought of publishing this book makes me sick to the stomach. I want it to be perfect. I want everything to be just right.

Is the cover design good enough? Did I write enough words? Did I write too much? Does it need more editing? Are there any really bad spelling errors? Have I said everything I wanted to say? Will people like this book? Will they hate it?

But that's the reason I wrote this book in the first place. The best ideas are worthless unless put into action. A badly written letter will always outperform a perfect letter that never gets sent.

I don't want to write the perfect book that never gets published. So here goes ...

Final Thoughts

I write these final words after coming back from the funeral of my wife's grandfather.

As I watched him being buried I stood in silence.

A different kind of silence. Not the silence that comes from a lack of sound but more of a silence that is louder than any sound you can make.

It was a silence of recognition. A reminder that life is short. Too short.

Too short for pondering, arguing, regretting, sitting on the fence, trying to impress, trying to always be right, doubting, asking "What if"?

We can only do our best. Our best is enough. Enough *is* enough.

At the end of it all, we are only left with our experiences.

Writing this book has been an experience. It isn't perfect. Far from it.

But good enough *is* enough... (for now)

About The Author

Daniel Gefen is a serial entrepreneur and founder of Gefen Media Group - a podcast production and booking agency helping clients build a loyal following through the power of podcasting. He is also the host of the top-rated podcast show called *'Can I Pick Your Brain?'* which has exceeded over 150,000 downloads and was named top 26 podcasts to listen to by CIO Magazine. He has interviewed over 100 thought leaders, Billionaires and celebrities.

In 2017, he was named one of the top 25 most influential influencers and has been featured in dozens of media publications including Forbes Inc, CIO, Influencive, Success Radio and over 70 leading podcasts.

Daniel lives with his wife Lorren and 4 children in the hills of Bet Shemesh, Israel.

You can listen to his show by searching for *'Can I Pick Your Brain?'* on iTunes or other podcast platforms.

You can also visit his personal website: www.DanielGefen.com

For further details about this book go to
www.TheSelfHelpAddict.com

Printed in Poland
by Amazon Fulfillment
Poland Sp. z o.o., Wrocław